LEGENDARY
ITALIAN
CARS

vmb
PUBLISHERS

CONTENTS

PREFACE
Giorgetto Giugiaro

TEXT
Enzo Rizzo

PROJECT EDITOR
Valeria Manferto De Fabianis

EDITORIAL COORDINATION
Laura Accomazzo - Giorgia Raineri

GRAPHIC DESIGN
Maria Cucchi

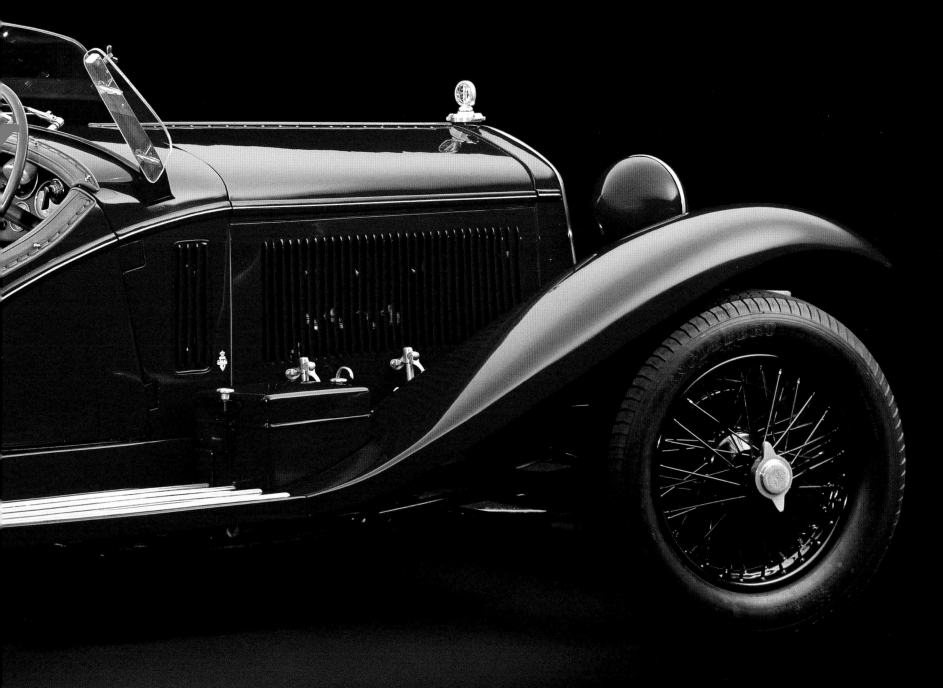

PREFACE

by Giorgetto Giugiaro

This volume simultaneously summarizes and describes the history of the Italian car, from its early beginnings to the modern day, revealing how both the concept and purpose of the engine-driven vehicle evolved so rapidly.

I found the following definition of the automobile in a 1920 edition by Pedretti, a scholarly *manual for the mechanic-chauffeur*:

"A self-propelling vehicle, or simply an automobile, is that mechanism that can move itself from one place to another at the will of a driver."

The engine, the long, impressive hood that housed it, and the thrilling speed that it released, all served to fuel the passion of four-wheel enthusiasts. People around the world fell in love with the new, the modern and everything that was the *car*.

The race to develop the car helped reduce the damage done by World War II, combined with the rapid construction of highways. The need for recovery and improvement was accompanied by the ability to dream big, and by faith in the power of technology. Dream cars were space-age cars, the premonition of new stylistic elements that would transform architecture, the landscape and our existential legends.

Pinin Farina crossed the Atlantic in the 1950s with hopes of beginning solid relations – starting with Nash Healey's project – with car manufacturers in Detroit. He was encouraged by Manhattan's mass media: the 1952 *New Yorker* defined his custom-built cars as *rolling sculptures*. And it was the *bodywork* and no longer the engine (albeit equipped with increasingly sophisticated performance) that made it possible for his cars to achieve widespread public acclaim.

Debates in the *Arte e Stile* and *Arte e Design* magazines spread to cultural newspapers. Alberto Giacometti posed the question in a 1957 edition of *Arts* as to whether or not *a relationship existed between the art of sculpture and the beauty of the automobile*. He concluded as follows:

"The automobile is an object that must be finished to operate and be used … A sculpture is not an object, rather a doubt, a question, an answer and as such can never be finished nor perfected … An automobile is only scrap iron when it breaks down, while a broken Chaldean sculpture in four pieces generates four sculptures".

Many Italian trademarks occupied the most prestigious platforms at the International Auto Shows in the 1960s, and *Italian style* conquered markets, admirers and imitators all over the world. As for the various racing disciplines, the winning combination of Italian designers and manufacturers with extremely talented racing drivers resulted in a collection of records that remain unbroken to this day.

The driver and passenger compartment, versatility, on-board information and service dominated the last decades of the twentieth century, which by overturning the relation between length, height and width of the means, provided the basis for minivans, vans and SUVs.

A definition of the car at the end of the century might have been:

"An automobile is a vehicle that allows people to move around conveniently, safely and quickly in order to meet their needs relating to work, the family and free time."

Like all of mankind's conquests, the history of the car is just as fascinating as it is fragile. It becomes part of a relationship between humans and nature, of a path embedded with traps, mysteries and effects that are sometimes noticeable only by the generations that follow.

The oil crisis – with obvious premonitions in the 1970s – and the global recession that started in late 2008, will rightfully be included in history books. The great reaction to the economic-financial upheaval started from new design bases, which will certainly recover the motor vehicle's charm by reinterpreting performance and formal content and standards for urban and outdoor use.

I venture to say that the next – but certainly not the last – definition of the car might be:

"The automobile is a vehicle for private or semi-public use, integrated within an intermodal viability and assisted system based on eco-sustainable principles, aiming to restrain the use of resources, energy consumption and atmospheric and noise pollution."

Freed – if not purified – by an honest sense of participation in the new realities created by the *homo faber*, let's venture out with *Legendary Italian Cars* and explore the development of the machines and innovative materials that have seduced us for more than a century.

Giorgetto Giugiaro was elected car designer of the 20th century in 1999. He is shown here working on the sketches of the Brera, a sporty Alfa Romeo that made its debut in 2005.

INTRODUCTION

The automobile is one of the symbols of *Made in Italy* around the world. Its success is the result of the genius and creativity of a select group of Italians, and a culture and history that has allowed the country to set the standard for good taste through great intuition and revolutionary creations.

It is true that the automobile was born in Germany, but it was in Italy that the first internal combustion engine was invented, in 1853, thanks to Eugenio Bersanti and Felice Matteucci. The first mass-produced eight-cylinder engine was used for the Isotta Fraschini Tipo 8 in 1919, the 1922 Lancia Lambda was the first vehicle in the world with independent wheels and a bearing body and structure, and the 1947 Cisitalia 202 by Pinin Farina became the standard for sports cars, just as Castagna's 1914 Alfa Romeo for Count Ricotti was the precursor to the modern minivan. And then you have the first Formula One World Championship, won by Alfa Romeo in 1950, and the world's first expressway, the Milano-Laghi built in 1923.

There is an incredible group of Italian personalities whose names are identified automatically with cars, many of which are still in business today: Enzo Ferrari, Vincenzo Lancia, Nicola Romeo, Ferruccio Lamborghini, Alfieri Macerati and Ettore Bugatti, to name a few. And then there are the car designers. In addition to Giorgetto Giugiaro, there was Pinin Farina and Bertone, Scaglietti and Zagato, plus others who worked for car manufacturers, such as Marcello Gandini or Flavio Bertoni who was behind many Citroën masterpieces.

Italian design engineers include Vittorio Jano for Alfa Romeo, and Dante Giacosa for the Fiat that introduced an industrial aspect to Italian cars and became a pioneer for the modern city car.

Last, but certainly not least, is Italy and motor racing. Italians are spoiled for choice in terms of race car drivers and winning cars, and their feats have contributed to a rich international history in this field.

This book tells the story of the Italian automobile through men, vehicles and ever-changing conditions. The chapters follow a chronological format that reviews social, economic and political factors, both in Italy and internationally, as well as the various eras of the Italian car and its development based on design generations and mechanical innovation.

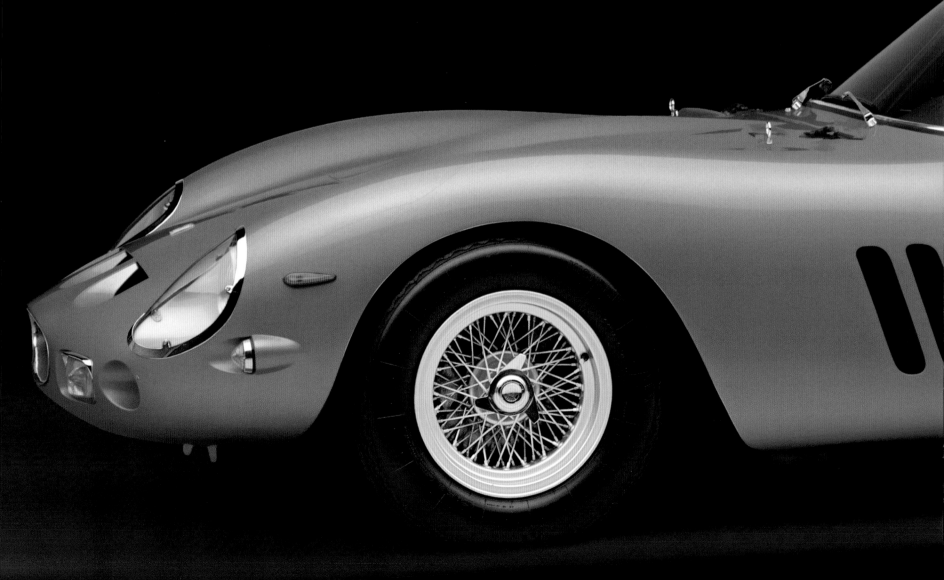

1 The Ferrari 308 Gts (Gran Turismo Spider) made its debut in 1977 with a rigid removable top that made it a coupe.

2-3 The 1995 Ferrari F50 celebrated the trademark's 50th anniversary. It boasted the best Formula One technology applied to a road-legal model.

4-5 The Maserati A6 GCS was presented in 1954 and immediately dominated races due to its speed and handling.

6-7 The Alfa Romeo 6C 2500 Villa d'Este was unofficially named after the Concours d'Elégance, which it won in 1949.

8-9 This Lamborghini Raptor Zagato was presented in Geneva in 1996. It had futuristic lines, 629 hp and reached speeds of up to 205 mph (330 km/h).

10-11 Elegant shapes for a sports car that undisputedly dominated races in the 1930s: The 6C 1750 Gran Sport, Alfa Romeo's signature model.

14-15 The 1962 250 Gto (Gran Turismo Omologato) is one of Ferrari's masterpieces. Sergio Scaglietti can be credited with its sensual and still modern shape.

16-17 This yellow Lancia Astura is from 1935. Its convertible version was often used as a presidential automobile.

18-19 The Isotta Fraschini Tipo 8 was manufactured from 1919 and was considered to be the most elegant, exclusive and sophisticated car in the world at the time. It was equipped with the first mass-produced eight-cylinder engine.

20-21 3600 units of the Ferrari 550 Maranello were manufactured between 1996 and 2002. It was equipped with a V12 5.5L (5474 cc), 485 hp engine that had a maximum speed of 199 mph (320 km/h).

22-23 This 2006 Ferrari P4/5 was the only one made and was produced for American James Glickenhaus by Carrozzeria Pininfarina based on an Enzo. Glickenhaus was also able to get his hands on the first Alfa Romeo 8C Competizione ever exported to the United States.

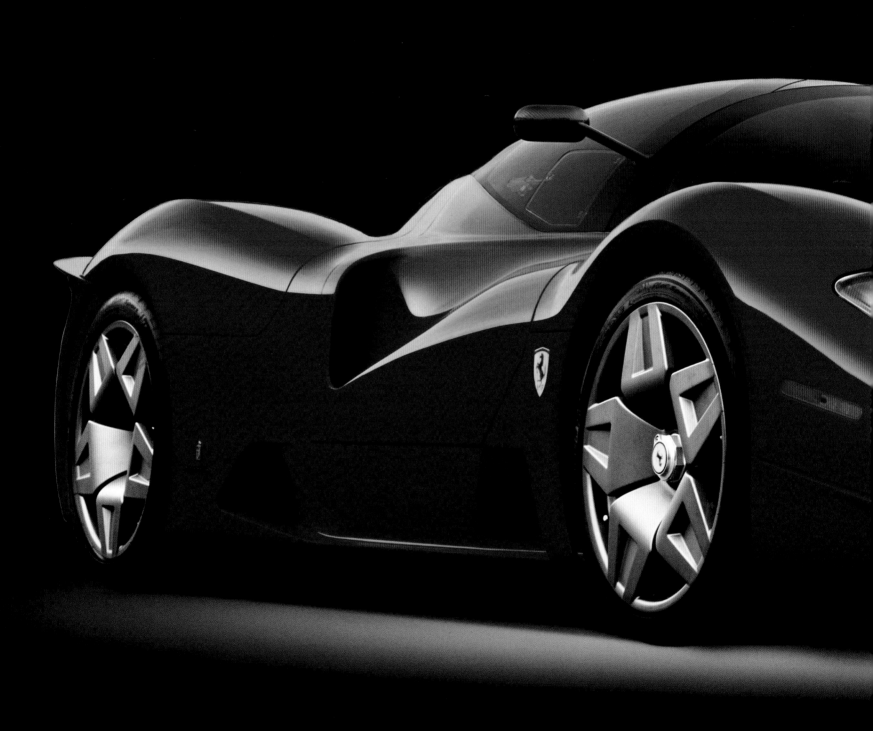

CHAPTER 1

Italy starts up its
engines:the first
manufacturers,
the early bodywork

The pioneers: from Benz and Daimler to Italian Menon and Bernardi

"I talians, a people of poets, saints and seafarers." And motorists. Right from the beginning of the car's history, Italians have written many of the most important pages. The first automobile driven by a spark-ignition engine was created in Germany in 1886, by technicians Karl Benz and Gottlieb Daimler, and the time was ripe for its fast distribution. So much so, in fact, that the birth of the automobile occurred only a short time thereafter, in France, England and Italy. Benz and Daimler respectively put three- and four-wheel vehicles, respectively, on the road at the same time but unbeknownst to each other. In 1924 they joined forces and two years later created Daimler-Benz, which we know today as Mercedes-Benz. These two men marked the starting point of the

24-25 Fiat founder, Senator Giovanni Agnelli with Luigi Storero, the owner of a factory that made bicycles, tricycles and quadricycles (such as the Phoenix on which they are photographed), after winning the race in Verona in 1899.

26-27 The drawings are of engines invented by Eugenio Barsanti and Felice Matteucci (from Lucca). The two Italians are considered the fathers of the spark-ignition engine, which was patented in England in 1854.

27 top The 1854 Bordino steam-operated carriage is actually on display in the Carlo Biscaretti Ruffia Auto Museum in Turin. It is basically a Landau, a type of carriage for several people that is not drawn by horses but is equipped with a rear water tank and an engine under the cabin.

car after a period of experimental models that moved on their own through the use of steam or electric traction, and the concept of the true automobile with an internal combustion engine came closer to reality.

In France, similar endeavors included Cugnot's three-wheel military vehicle, created in 1769 to transport artillery, and the steam versions that increasingly resembling automobiles from the sec-

ond half of the 19th century, created by Amédée Bollée, Léon Serpollet and Georges Bouton. These gentlemen founded a company in 1881 with the eclectic Jules-Albert de Dion, the founder of the Automobile Club of France, the world's first automobile association and a depositary of well-known mechanical patents that are still in use, such as the De Dion wheel axle bridge. Britain's precocious industrialization sustained a certain confidence and steam traction was used to drive public carriages. Several manufacturers even drove around in single models they had invented, like Walter Hancock in his 1838 phaeton four-seater. However, electric traction was preferred in the United States. The first electric taxis circulated in New York in 1894, and there was also the torpedo-shaped *La Jamais Contente* (Never Satisfied) driven by Camille Jenatzy, which reached speeds in excess of 62 miles per hour (100 kilometers per hour) in 1899. Preference was purely a matter of practicality; with steam, it took one hour to heat up approximately 26 gallons (100 liters) in the tank and create pressure in the engine, not to mention frequent stops at a friend's place or a public fountain to fill up with water.

In Italy, steam provided the drive to a two-cylinder engine mounted on the Bordino Carriage, a Landau carriage created in 1854 at a military base in Turin, which is now actually on display in Turin's Biscaretti Museum. The vehicle was named after Virginio Bordino, an officer in the Sardinian army. Bordino made use of the experience he gained in London, where he was sent to study methods of transportation that could be of service to the army. Despite an initial preference for electric or steam engines, however, the spark ignition engine was chosen for the automobile because it was not difficult to use nor did it require a lot of strength to start up with a crank (especially for women). It was also quiet, didn't vibrate and didn't require gears. However, continuous experimentation and never-ending improvements in efficiency, functionality and ease of use ultimately led to the distribution of units equipped with internal combustion engines. The fathers of the spark-ignition engine are considered to be Italians

Eugenio Bersanti and Felice Matteucci. These two gentlemen registered a paper at the Georgofili Academy in Florence in 1853 related to the construction of their spark-ignition engine, which was patented the following year in England. In 1882 a Veronese professor of mechanical construction at the University of Padua named Enrico Zeno Bernardi patented a gas-operated spark-ignition engine. It was a single-cylinder 0.1 liter (130 cubic centimeters) engine with less than one horsepower, used initially to operate small machine tools. In 1884 he assembled it on a wooden tricycle for his son Lauro and, 10 years later, he assembled it on a three-wheel vehicle, the *Triciclo*. In the meantime, he obtained 0.6L (600 cc) with 1.5-2.5 hp. It required two pounds (800 grams) of gas per hour and could reach between 17 and 22 mph (28 and 35 km/h), depending on the horsepower.

Another year would pass, however, before the birth of the first Italian automobile. It was 1895, in Roncade in the Italian province of Treviso, that craftsman Carlo Menon built a small, four-wheel vehicle with a single-cylinder, air-cooled, 0.5L (490 cc), 3.5 hp De Dion-Bouton engine. It was named the Rebus and was the first Italian automobile to be mass produced. Menon subsequently fine tuned and built the engine on his own, obtaining good results in terms of reliability and solidity. He was able to produce 20 or so automobiles (one still "operated" by his heirs) until 1902, when the production of this small vehicle become secondary to producing velocipedes, weapons and ammunition.

Bernardi's vehicle was also mass produced. The Miari, Giusti & C. company was established in Padua in 1896 and over the next six years it manufactured approximately 100 between Triciclo (60 or so, five of which still exist) and Quadriciclo units. The latter was a four-wheel version that had the same engine size and horsepower as the three-wheel version but the differential was located on the rear wheels. Other differences included a more complex steering system and a choice of bodywork, including a two-seater (side by side) for the Triciclo, an open version with an extended wheel-

It should be pointed out that during the first years of its life, the automobile benefitted from those same mechanical inventions (electronics aside, naturally) that have reached us today through natural evolution. The protagonists of the four-wheel revolution come from Europe and the United States. Remember that the automobile was born in Germany, developed in France, and became an adult in the United States, and that Italy and England played a very important role in all of this. Specifically, Italy continued to follow in the wake of technology and, as well as the spark-ignition engine,

and foreign (Mercedes-Benz, Duesemberg) automakers. Another master was Turinese Giacinto Ghia (born in 1887) whose body shop initially started producing bodywork for wealthy clients and then, when he separated from his partner in the workshop they had opened in 1915, he devoted his time to working with Alfa Romeo, Lancia and Fiat by creating an open sports car based on a 1929 6C 1500, the Augusta and the Balilla. Ugo Zagato was born in 1890 in Gavello, in the Italian province of Rovigo. He had a different background to that of the other car designers, having studied at Carrozze-

base (distance between the wheel axles), an additional rear seat, windshield, luggage and umbrella compartment and a four-seater.

Thanks to Menon and Bernardi, the Veneto region became the birthplace of the Italian automobile. Another notable name was Gaetano Rossi, the owner of Lanerossi (industry in the wool sector in Piovene Rocchette in the Italian province of Vicenza). As the first motorist in Italy as of January 2, 1893, Rossi received the Peugeot vis-à-vis chassis number 25 by train, which he had ordered in August 1892. For 14 months this industrialist from Vicenza was the only person in Italy to drive around in an automobile, until Ginori from Florence arrived in February of 1894 with his flaming Panhard-Levasseur.

many four-wheel innovations also flew the Italian flag. This is, of course, in addition to the style and elegance of the shapes, which remains and will always remain Italian, largely thanks to figures who never received the credit they deserved. One of these was Carlo Castagna. He was born in 1845 and can be defined as the *carriage and bodywork man,* as he experienced the transition from transportation by horse to the automobile. He started working at the age of nine as an apprentice in the Paolo Mainetti carriage factory in Milan, but his creativity and ability led him to establish Carrozzeria Castagna in 1906. This activity was continued by his sons, Ercole and Emilio, who *dressed* the chassis of the most important Italian (Alfa Romeo, Isotta Fraschini, Lancia)

ria Varesina (a bus manufacturer) and at Officine Aeronautiche Pomilio in Turin. This different career path led him to develop his own style, which, years later after World War I, would be expressed in automobiles for Alfa Romeo, Lancia, Abarth and Maserati, in addition to the famous coupe on an Aston Martin DB4 GT chassis – one of the great post-WWII masterpieces. Another genius of shapes was Flaminio Bertoni from Masnago in the Italian province of Varese (born 1903), who, like many other Italians, plied his trade abroad. He was responsible for the shape of the Citroën Traction Avant, the first and only example of a model to be approved on the basis of a small Plasticine model rather than on a design. André Citroën was so enthused by Bertoni's work that he immediately gave orders to put it into production. Bertoni's other masterpieces included the 2 CV, DS and Ami 6, which were also designed for Citroën. Finally, there was Mario Revelli di Beaumont, who was born in Rome in 1907 and specialized in aerodynamic research. This made him highly sought after in the 1930s when this subject became the *leitmotif* for production models. He collaborated with Carrozzerie Viotti, Farina, Ghia, Bertone, Pininfarina, Fiat, Simca, and General Motors and also created many bodywork elements, all of which featured the much-missed adjustable quarter vent window.

28 Car designer Giacinto Ghia behind the wheel. In 1915 he and a partner opened a workshop to build bodies. The two split 10 years later and Ghia went on to found Carrozzeria Ghia and to supply chassis for Alfa Romeo, Lancia and Fiat customers.

28-29 This curious bicycle with a "trailer," photographed in New York on December 28, 1894, was designed so that the cyclist did not have to pedal, as it was driven by a gas-operated spark engine, the precursor to the current engines created by Italian professor Enrico Bernardi.

From craftsmen to the assembly line, the industrial dimension was born

Automobiles are now almost automatically associated with factories and assembly lines, a preconception that has more recently been combined with automation and robots. Like all products destined for mass production, the beginnings almost always lie in making a craftsman's dimensions able to sustain reduced numbers. As for the Italian car, Menon and then especially Bernardi started a substantial series of small enterprises to fine tune, experiment and produce controlled quantities of this new means of transportation, destined for the few people who could afford them. Interest increased and grew world-wide, leading to an industrial revolution of sorts in Italy at the end of the 19th century. The first factories included Fabbrica Italiana Automobili Torino (Fiat) in 1899 in the front line. Other important manufacturers were established in Fiat's wake, such as Isotta Fraschini in 1900, Itala in 1904, Bianchi and Lancia in 1907 and Alfa in 1910.

These manufacturers inherited the legacy of a series of small manufactures (at the beginning of the 20th century there were 96) including Star in Turin, Marchand in Piacenza and Florentia in Flo-

rence. They were also highly regarded abroad, where the competition was already fierce, abundant and structured from an industrial perspective. For example, in 1899, there were 888 manufacturers in Europe and 1298 mechanics (known today as garages), led by France with 619 manufacturers, 1095 mechanics and 2000 vehicles in circulation. These numbers may seem trivial today, but back then they were a significant expression of this phenomenon. In Italy, where the car was truly believed in, 300 vehicles were manufactured and approximately 100 cars were on the streets in the year that Fiat was established.

30-31 An Italian family immortalized on a Fiat during an outing in 1908. The chauffeur was a fundamental figure because, in addition to preparing and driving the vehicle, he also took care of maintenance.

31 Fiat founder Giovanni Agnelli (right) together with the long-distance racing team and driver Felice Nazzaro, whose vehicle dominated road races during the first 20 years of the twentieth century.

The company was established on July 11, 1899 at the offices of Banco Sconto e Sete by a group of wealthy and far-sighted enthusiasts who rightfully believed in the evolution of the automobile. The group comprised of 30 individuals whose initial capital amounted to 800,000 Lira, divided into 4000 shares worth 200 Lira each. The members of the Board of Directors were Scarfiotti (chairman), Agnelli (president), Biscaretti di Ruffia, Ceriana, Damerino, Di Bricherasio, Ferrero di Ventimiglia, Goria Ratti and Racca. These were among the best known figures and personalities from the city of Turin, a first-class administrative and business center at the end of the century. The mechanical industry up to that time was linked to and fragmented among a series of workshops and small laboratories. Fiat was able to change the city's way of life, offer new economic prospects and free up money that would otherwise have remained confined to personal patrimonies. Fiat's headquarters were set up in Corso Dante in 1900. The original factory covered a surface area equal to 14,352 square yards (12,000 square meters) and employed 35 workers. The first vehicle was already being manufactured; the 3½ HP, two- or three-seater *duc* with a two-cylinder, 0.7L (679 cc), 4.2 hp rear engine. In other words, it was a motorized carriage with a 5-foot (1.47 meter) wheelbase that was 5 ft (1.47 m) wide and weighed 926 pounds (420 kilograms), designed by Aristide Faccioli with bodywork by Marcello Alessio and assembled in Ceirano's workshop. This was the same project Ceirano used to obtain the Welleyes, the bicycles manufactured by the Turinese company of the same name. Welleyes was founded in 1898 by Giovanni Battista Ceirano, Emanuele di Bricherasio, Attilio Calligaris, Pietro Fenoglio and Cesare Goria Gatti at the same address where Giuseppe Lancia, the father of Vincenzo and creator of the automaker, lived. The 3½ HP vehicle stood out for its rear wheels (larger than the front ones), wooden rims and its wooden chassis, the leaf spring and support fittings for the mechanical section of which were reinforced with iron. The vehicle was driven by a large lever with two knobs used as a handle and it was capable of reaching 22 mph (35 km/h). The driver sat in the back seat and might have visibility problems if a passenger was on the front bench. A parchment trademark bore the hand-written company name and the progressive vehicle number. Sold for 4200 Lira, 26 units were manufactured, two of which are on display at the Museum of the Automobile in Turin and at the Ford Museum in Dearborn (USA).

34 This glamorous advertising poster was created in 1899 by Turinese artist and poster designer Giovanni Battista Carpanetto. It advertised the new 3½ HP, Fiat's first vehicle.

34-35 This 1911 photograph shows several chassis ready or being finished in the vehicle assembly area in the Fiat factory at Corso Dante. The most modern mechanical technology was used here and the factory employed 35 workers.

The 6 HP was Fiat's second car and the first manufactured in the factory in Corso Dante. It was 1910 and the entire decade was devoted to manufacturing medium- to high-powered, right-hand drive models that provided the best roadside visibility. The term production in this case only refers to the chassis, because bodywork was assigned to third parties. Interestingly, tires were accessories and incurred a separate cost because they were very expensive and fragile. The roads back then didn't help much either. The 6 HP was derived from the 3½ HP, but was more of an automobile in terms of displacement (1.1L or 1100 cc), the existence of a reverse gear, the option of a steering wheel, and its shape, as the larger chassis offered a choice of bodywork. There was also the Corsa version, which reached 37 mph (60 km/h), while the 10 HP (also derived from the 6 HP) had a larger body by Alessio. The 8 HP was a different mat-

ter. It was the last one designed by Faccioli and participated in the first Automobile Tour of Italy. This was the first car with a front engine equipped with vertical rather than horizontal cylinders. Forty-one units of this vehicle were produced, which was equipped with a 1.1L (1082 cc) engine, smooth gears made in France and duc or phaeton bodywork by Alessio. In addition to being the first car by Giovanni Enrico (who replaced Faccioli), the 12 HP was also the first model to be highly regarded abroad (especially in France) and provided Fiat with considerable international exposure. The credit for this success was also due to the vehicle's innovations, such as the front, four-cylinder engine placed in two vertical twin-blocks and a honeycomb radiator that also added a touch of style to the vehicle's front end. The vehicle was 11 ft (3.27 m) long, equipped with a 3.8L (3768 cc), 16 hp engine, reached 43 mph (70 km/h) and required 0.22 gallons (1 L) to travel three miles (5 km). The car, of which 106 units were produced, was intended for long trips and cost 12,000 Lira. Giovanni Agnelli became president of Fiat in 1902, a position he deserved thanks to his strong managerial qualities and uncontainable entrepreneurial spirit. He believed in communication and in promoting his vehicles, so much so that the Automobile Tour of Italy, which he organized, finished up at the Convention Center in Milan and brought him great international success. The company was listed on the stock exchange the following year, confirming its move towards expansion and a specific interest in foreign markets. By becoming a public company, Fiat benefitted from the stock exchange boom in this sector. This not only made it possible to expand into international markets, but also to overcome the great car crisis of 1907-1908 that had brought many manufacturers to their knees.

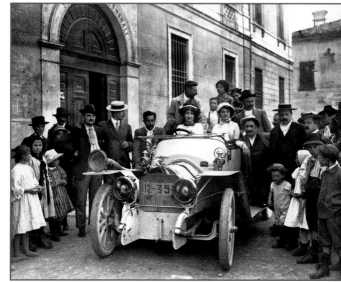

Exports to the United States started in 1903 (Fiat Automobile Co. was established there in 1908), the same year that the 24-32 HP made its debut. It was available in three wheelbases (short, medium and long) and its engine size reached 7.4L (7363 cc). It was a preview of a high-powered car and targeted elite owners, including the House of Savoy. In 1906 it evolved into the 24-40 HP and the following year into the 28-40 HP. This was the road-legal version of the 16-20 HP presented in 1903 and used in the Targa Florio race, which 12 months later became the 16-24 HP and, in 1908, the 18-24 HP.

It featured several mechanical improvements, such as air-compressed ignition, and was considered a medium-powered model (4.2L or 4200 cc) and, like the 24-32 HP, was also available with Landaulet bodywork. Then the 60 HP was created with export and rich markets in mind. This high-powered vehicle, which exceeded 10.0L (10,000 cc), was available with various wheelbase configurations that allowed it to transport up to seven passengers. The sporty two-seater version had a better performing engine, which was initially able to reach 103 mph (165 km/h) and, in 1905, the Tipo Record version, which broke 124 mph (200 km/h) for the first time in automobile history. Another version was the 50-60 HP with a six-cylinder engine (rather than 4 cylinders), ordered by the King of Spain, while the evolutions of the 60 HP into 35-45 HP and 35-50 HP all headed in the direction of America and Australia.

This brings us to 1910, the end of Fiat's first decade, during which it had become a company of considerable size, with 2500 employees and an annual production of 1215 vehicles, a far cry from the 268 vehicles it manufactured in 1904. Its journey towards expansion brought it to the Great War having manufactured 4644 cars, half of the entire national production. Before 1915, Fiat took three more important steps.

The year 1908 marked the debut of the Fiat 1 Fiacre, used for urban public transportation. The success of this vehicle was not only measured by the 1600 units produced, but also by its approval by several other large foreign cities such as New York, London and Paris. This was largely thanks to its reduced displacement (2.0L or 2009 cc), which provided adequate performance and the ability to transport up to five people plus their baggage. Starting in 1910, the models were given different names beginning with Tipo followed by a progressive number from one to seven.

In 1912 came the Zero, a cornerstone in technological evolution not only for Fiat, but for the entire Italian automotive industry. In fact, 2000 units of this car were manufactured by 1915, but more importantly, it was mass produced on assembly lines, from the chassis to the bodywork and mechanics. This was thanks to the exchange of technology with Ford in the United States. On one of his overseas trips to the American company's workshops, Agnelli saw for himself what was meant by so-called 'Fordism,' the industrial production system created by Henry Ford and realized in an assembly line, an automated handling system connecting all processing operations of an automobile's individual components in sequence with the assembly procedures. The effect that this method had in reducing the final price of the product was decisive. The reductions in costs and time were just as impressive as the increase in production. Imagine, Ford went from manufacturing 34,550 Model T vehicles in 1911 to 248,307 in 1913, while the time required to make a car decreased from 750 minutes to only 93.

Fiat drew on this revolutionary production system completely and, after combining it with several Taylorist methods, applied it to the Zero, with thrilling results. The car's original selling price decreased from 8000 Lira to 6900 Lira in 1913 because production costs had benefitted from initial amortization. Initially, the Zero came in a single version, equipped with a 1.8L (1847 cc) engine and a single, torpedo-shaped body that seated four.

38-39 This marvelous 1907 red Fiat 130 HP was equipped with a 16.3L (16.286 cc), 130 hp engine and reached a maximum speed of 99 mph (160 km/h). Three cars were lined up at the 1907 French Grand Prix driven by Vincenzo Lancia, Louis Wagner and Felice Nazzaro, who won the race.

39 top A 1912 red Fiat Zero. This was an important model for Fiat and the Italian automobile industry. It was the first car built entirely - from the chassis to the bodywork — on an assembly chain and therefore intended for mass production.

Giovanni Agnelli appointed the design of the radiator to a certain Battista Farina, otherwise known as Pinin. Born in Turin of November 2, 1893, Pinin was already working in his brother Giovanni's car repair shop at age 12, and at 18 he met Agnelli. Fiat commissioned Pinin with the Zero's torpedo-shaped bodywork line, which had been realized by his brother. Pinin then went to the United States to learn new construction techniques and later started creating models, many of which met with international acclaim and were also commissioned by foreign manufacturers. He was another well known figure, envied by the world, and an undisputed standard bearer of Italian style around the globe.

The Fiat Zero was manufactured until 1915 and, towards the end of its honored and revolutionary career, it benefitted from the expansion of the range to satisfy those who wanted to personalize it, aristocrats who didn't want the same car everyone else had. This concept has accompanied the entire history of the automobile and become its leitmotif, especially today when it seems that (almost) everything has been invented for the car. Another analogy with the present is that the Zero was Fiat's first seed in what would become its DNA: an automaker specialized in economy cars. Speed was another important component in those days. In 1912 in Long Island, New York, the Fiat 300 HP Record (though the effective power was only 290 HP) reached 180 mph (290 km/h) and established a new world record for the mile. However, from a pre-war perspective, the application of mass production was also useful to Fiat for satisfying military job orders. In 1914 Fiat produced 20,000 18BL trucks, in 1915 it manufactured engines for MAS motor torpedo boats and in the next two years it turned to airplane propulsion systems, not to mention actual aircraft, rescue means and even bullets. In 1917, Fiat had 15,000 employees and produced 19,184 motor vehicles. These considerable quantities led to the start of construction (the previous year) of the new Lingotto factory based on Giacomo Mattè Trucco's project. When construction was completed in 1922, it was the largest and most modern factory in all of Europe.

40-41 An evocative and powerful representation of the Fiat factory in Turin in 1917. A giant male figure uses his manual abilities to mould metals that will become automobile chassis.

From Isotta Fraschini to Bianchi, Bugatti and the Ceirano brothers

Fiat was the leader during this initial phase of the Italian four-wheel scene, followed by a series of manufacturers who contributed to Italy's reputation as an automobile-maker throughout the world. However, some of these were short-lived because they couldn't keep up with the technological pace, while others such as Lancia and Alfa/Alfa Romeo continued through the decades until their encounter with Fiat.

Isotta Fraschini and its 50 years of history gained a place of honor in the automobile world. The brand made a brief comeback in the 1990s, but it was a flash in the pan and did not give credit to the efforts and passion of Cesare Isotta and his brothers Vincenzo, Oreste and Antonio Fraschini, who had established the company in Milan back in 1900. The brothers had started their activities before that, selling Renault vehicles that they equipped with De Dion engines, and then as importers and assemblers of Renaults. Two years later it was the turn of small vehicles equipped with Aster and De Dion engines and then, in 1903, the first chassis and engine completely produced by Isotta Fraschini Milan. This was the Tipo 24 HP, many of which were exported

and became known internationally, thanks to its solidity and reliability as well as its elegant bodywork. The arrival in 1905 of technical director Giustino Cattaneo, a brilliant engineer with experience gained in Florentia and Züst, sent the company in a very precise technical direction, which included innovations and developments in the area of racing. The company became the first in the world to patent a front-wheel brake system (until then, brakes had been at the back), a project it later granted under license to foreign manufacturers. Fraschini also participated in the production of the first race car, the 100 hp, 17.0L (17,000 cc) Tipo D 100 HP Corsa. The sporting successes in the years that followed included the Targa

Florio with Trucco and Maserati, the speed record by the 40 HP at Long Island – a three-hour average of 65 mph (105 km/h) – and the Tipo B 28-35 HP, Tipo FE, Tipo KM and Tipo TM vehicles. These achievements helped the company establish a reputation that brought recognition to the brand and led to a certain corporate success. This was enhanced by the entry of the French with De Dietrich, who bought the rights to manufacturer 500 Isotta Fraschini chassis. Starting in 1911, the company began producing airplane and airship propulsion systems, an activity that became just as important as manufacturing cars, which it continued to do both during World War I and after from a racing perspective.

42-43 The 1913 Isotta Fraschini Tipo Km was driven by a four-cylinder, twin-shaft 0.7L (700 cc), 100 hp engine with valves in the cylinder head, and capable of reaching 93 mph (150 km/h). Seven were manufactured by the Milanese manufacturer.

43 top Harry Grant took control of the Vanderbilt Cup on his Isotta just after the start of the race. The American driver won this race in 1909 and 1910.

44-45 Ettore Bugatti on a 1907 Deutz Tip 9C owned and driven by Prince Henry. Bugatti worked for the German manufacturer in 1907 and 1908.

45 Bugatti's advertising poster with the classic blue that characterized the company's vehicles. It dates back to 1927, a marvelous period for the brand that resulted in unforgettable models such as the Type 35 or the Type 41 Royale.

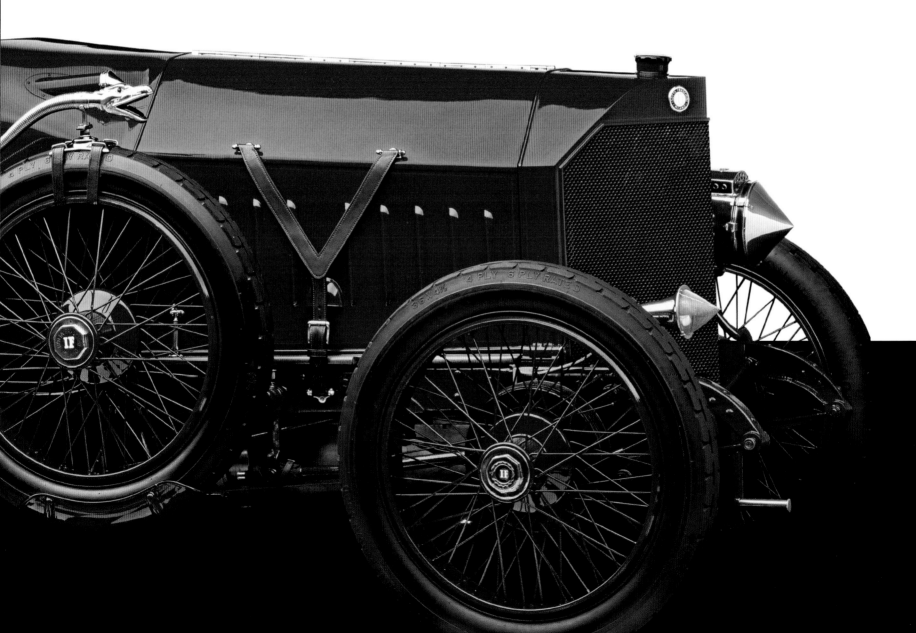

Another noble brand was Bugatti & Gulinelli, even though the history of one of the two partners was mixed in with French history. This is how the four-wheel adventure of Milanese genius Ettore Bugatti started. In 1900 he was working on an automobile project while still an employee for Stucchi Prinetti. He showed his project to the Counts Gulinelli of Ferrara in the hope of obtaining financing. Once he received approval, Bugatti produced a model in the counts' villa in Monte Santo, and it was displayed in the Ricordi stand at the International Sports Show in Milan in 1901. It was a success, as Bugatti was awarded the grand prize by the jury and the Coppa Città Milano. This vehicle was different from the models people were used to seeing; it was an open two-seater with circular seats, had a refined-looking front end, a water-cooled, four-vertical-cylinder engine with poppet-valve distribution and four gears plus reverse. The death in 1901 of one of the Counts of Gulinelli complicated the life of this revolutionary model, which was purchased by De Dietrich, who also hired Bugatti. This was just the beginning for Ettore, who waited a few more years before starting his own business and astonishing the world with his inventiveness. But the seed had been planted. As with Isotta Fraschini, Bugatti (as a brand) also made a comeback in the 1990s and, just like the other Milanese automaker, no credit was given to its unforgettable founder.

Bianchi's first model dates back to 1902. The company was established in 1897, for the purpose of manufacturing motor vehicles, by Edoardo Bianchi, a bicycle manufacturer whose brand is still among the world leaders. This is due to the spirit of innovation and great technical enterprise of its founder, who invented the transmission chain, tire and women's frame for bicycles. It was only logical that Bianchi would also make an attempt at powered vehicles and, after a tricycle with a De Dion-Bouton engine, a quadricycle obtained from the four-wheeled version and a motorcycle, it was the turn of the first automobile completely manufactured by this Milanese brand. It soon became a range, offering six models that could mount either Aster or De Dion engines. A double chassis to protect the mechanics and elegant bodywork embellished with precious materials and parts added value to these vehicles, the price of which also included home assistance and one or two days of driving school. The short distance from the road to the race track was a logical step for its brilliant founder; he asked for collaboration from expert technicians, and numerous successes in Italy and abroad soon followed. But Bianchi wanted to run

the real race with Fiat and during the years prior to World War I, the Milanese manufacturer became Fiat's main competitor. This was the reason for models such as the Tipo A intended to compete against the Turinese Zero, while models like the S had a single version and continued the logic of standardization and curbing costs and final prices. The other more refined and elegant models were less successful due to their high production costs. During the war, Bianchi was also involved in manufacturing vehicles for the army and aero engines under license. This reconversion wasn't fatal, as its core business remained bicycles and motorcycles, but automobiles continued to be successful and more than a match for Fiat.

46-47 This racing vehicle was photographed in Brescia in 1905 while it was leaving an auto garage after ordinary maintenance checks.

47 Giovanni Negri, the founder

of the famous Italian photography studio, was fascinated by the charm of this new, revolutionary means of transportation. He is photographed here in 1908 with his wife and chauffeur.

This Milan-Turin rivalry brings us back to the Piedmont capital (Turin) where Ceirano Matteo & C. Vetture Marca Itala was founded in 1904. Matteo Ceirano was restless when it came to cars. The brother of Giovanni Battista (the founder of the Turinese company that produced the Welleyes, which in turn resembled the first Fiat), he participated in the Susa-Moncenisio race with an Itala 24 HP to win the category. This success was the first of a series, which convinced many investors to believe in him and to appoint Alberto Ballocco as the technical director of Itala Fabbrica di Automobili in July 1904. Ballocco presented the 100 HP (15.0L or 15,000 cc), 50 HP, 18 HP and the 40 HP, which won the Targa Florio. But it was the Beijing-Paris long distance car rally in 1907 that gave rise to international honors for Itala and all of Italy. Successful races led to the expansion of the company, which in 1911 had 1250 employees and manufactured 750 vehicles. There were many technical novelties, such as the transmission shaft (rather than the chain-belt transmission) or the V8 engine with rotary valve gears, which allowed the propulsion system to operate silently and smoothly. This device was called Avalve, and gave its name to the 50 HP model produced from 1913 to 1916. The war years arrived and Itala worked with other companies headed by Scat (Società Ceirano Automobili Torino). The latter was established in 1905 by Giovanni Ceirano to produce cutting-edge models, which led to many racing successes. Among these were victories by a 25-35 HP Corsa in the 1911, 1912 and 1914 Targa Florio races. Itala and its associates were also involved in the production of 3000 aero engines under Hispano-Suiza license. At the end of the war, only half the engines were delivered and the remaining 1500 were no longer needed (the Italian government was the primary buyer), which led to a crisis that Turinese Itala would endure for a long time.

48-49 This doorless 1906 convertible Itala was perfectly at ease along the exclusive streets of Monaco. These were the years when the Turinese manufacturer produced both touring and racing models with the 40 HP, which won the 1906 Targa Florio.

ITALA

Modello 56 15-20 HP
Modello 50 25-30 HP
Modello 51 SPORT 25-45 HP
Modello TAXI 1924 · 14-18 HP

FABBRICA AUTOMOBILI TORINO

49 top A child gives directions to the driver of a streamlined, sporty Itala. This was the advertising poster created in 1924 to increase sales for the 50 and 51 Sport models, the six-cylinder 56 and even taxis.

49 bottom This Itala 50 torpedo-shaped vehicle dates back to 1920. The car was manufactured between 1919 and 1926. Elegant yet solid, most of this vehicle's chassis were sold abroad, especially in Australia.

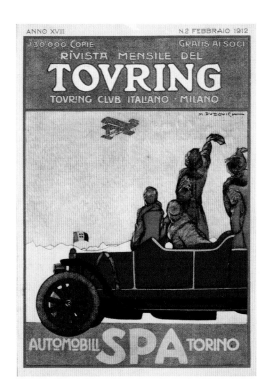

In any event, the Ceirano family was among the leading protagonists of the Italian automobile at the beginning of the 20th century and brought prestige to Piedmont, which after Veneto, was the most receptive region to four-wheelers. Matteo left Ceirano in 1905 to establish SPA (Società Piemontese Automobili) in 1906 with Michele Ansaldi, an expert in the field of industrial organization and production systems. Matteo was responsible for all model designs up to 1918. The first included the 28-40 HP and the 60-70 HP with a

transmission shaft or cardan-shaft transmission, which were quite successful at the International Exhibition in Turin in 1907. Ceirano was later reported by Itala for unfair competition because he had built a factory not very far from his former home. But the anxieties of this restless technician were especially due to financial problems that could only improve when SPA merged with Fabbrica Ligure Automobili Genova (Flag) in 1908. This merger led to the manufacture of trucks to satisfy job orders from various government ministries. However, the new production line did not distract SPA from its racing successes, which translated into long-distance car rallies, endurance tests and demonstrations of the solidity of their vehicles, which certainly did not have the benefit of today's roads, technology and widespread assistance. In addition to all of this was the aeronautic branch, with production of engines under the management of Aristide Faccioli, Fiat's original technical manager. With the arrival of the war, the corporate background also changed as SPA faced the conflict without its two founding partners, who left the company. The company turned to producing engines for airplanes, but especially for heavy-duty vehicles with the arrival of important supply orders, including some from the Russian government. Many of these vehicles were equipped with the chassis from the 35-50 HP, produced from 1912 to 1916 with a four-cylinder, 7.6L (7604 cc) engine and a short or long wheelbase. Several were also sold in China, confirming its solidity. Delayed payments, however, led to a crisis at SPA and the Genoese ownership left the company.

The automobile manufacturing that Italy had become so highly regarded for abroad, in turn became a market for foreign manufacturers, including the French company Darracq and Eng-

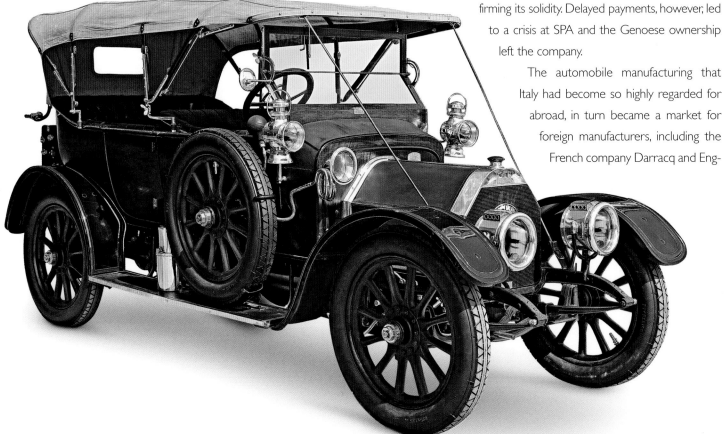

TORPEDO SU CHASSIS "SPA" 25–30 HP

land's Daimler. Darracq established an Italian branch in Naples in 1906 to bypass customs barriers and thus sell its vehicles in Italy. The partnership included engineers, personalities and Italian banks and allowed Italian Darracq to assemble the small 8-10 HP, which was very successful on the other side of the Alps and throughout Europe. In 1907 the factories were moved to Portello in Milan and production also included vehicles with four-cylinder engines and approximately 15 hp. However, sales were not overwhelming; the 8-10 HP was heavily influenced by Italian competition, Darracq left in 1909 and the factory in Milan was taken over by an emerging company named Alfa. As for Daimler, the De Luca brothers from Naples attempted to distribute the well known English models in Italy, which led to the creation of De Luca Daimler in 1906. Eight hundred workers were employed in this factory, which covered over 646,000 square feet (60,000 square meters), to manufacture the chassis of four models and assemble the mechanical components received from the parent company. But the most interesting vehicle was the 1908 Auto Mista, especially when viewed through today's eyes and in terms of automobile problems tied to the environment and reducing emissions. This was in fact a hybrid vehicle with two engines; one was gas-operated (6.8L or 6786 cc) and the other was electrically operated and had a battery that housed 80 elements. It was especially designed by the De Luca brothers to spark interest from public administration. However, this forerunner to the hybrid car was not accepted very well by the English, who preferred gas-operated models. Then in 1909, Daimler failed to comply with its contract to accept the chassis that had already been manufactured, leading to a crisis for the Neapolitan company. The following year, it interrupted production and became Daimler Italiana. This was not much of a solution and the company was forced to close down at the end of 1910.

The first steps by Lancia and Alfa

The Lancia headquarters and workshop were opened on November 29, 1906 in a few buildings in Turin that had once belonged to Itala. Its founders were Vincenzo Lancia and Claudio Fogolin, a friend from Fiat and test driver. Vincenzo was born in Fobello (Vercelli) on August 24, 1881 and was the third son of industrialist Giuseppe Lancia, who had run a solid, prosperous preserves company. Vincenzo's love for mechanics led to him being hired at the age of 16 in

the Ceirano brothers' workshop (located on the first floor at Corso Vittorio Emanuele 9, home to the Lancia family) and participating in the creation of the Welleyes. His father did not approve of his career choice, having hoped his son would become a lawyer. But Vincenzo was very determined and when Fiat took over Ceirano and the related patents in 1899 for 30,000 Lira, it employed Vincenzo as a test driver. He later became an official racing driver as he was quite

capable behind the wheel, so much so that in 1900 he won his first race, in Padua, and was generally among the front-runners in later races. But the podium didn't satisfy him, which brings us back to November 29, 1906, when Vincenzo and his friend Fogolin opened up their workshop at Via Ormea, ready to make their dreams come true and to create a vehicle bearing Vincenzo's name. He left Fiat but relations with Agnelli remained excellent, so much so that Giovanni gave the

newly established company 50,000 Lira. A fire hindered production of the first vehicle, but in September of 1907 the Tipo 51, or Alfa 12 HP, was born. This model was not very large, but stood out for its elaborate mechanics and elevated specific hp, considering the 2.5L (2543 cc) four-cylinder engine produced 24 hp. Despite its contained size, the chassis could not be removed from the workshop, so Lancia and Fogolin had to widen the door with a pickaxe. This incident truly explains Lancia's passion and love for the automobile, as though that chassis were the center of the universe and nothing else mattered. The first vehicle already had a name in Greek letters that has always identified Lancia vehicles. Vincenzo's brother Giuseppe Lancia, an arts teacher and highly regarded Greek scholar, was responsible for this choice. From Limousines and Landaulets to double phaetons and two-seater race cars, Alfa stood out for its excellent performance and ease of handling without compromising on outfitting. This explains why most of the 108 units they manufactured were exported to the United States and Australia. As usual, quality was recognized. It is no coincidence that American millionaire John D. Rockefeller was seen driving a Lancia Theta, the flagship *par excellence* for on-board comfort and luxury as well as performance. The likes of Isotta Fraschini would be needed to create an alternative to the Turinese limousine.

But before Alfa terminated its cycle in 1909, Lancia proposed the Dialfa, a name taken from the Greek alphabet with the prefix "di" or "tri" (two or three times), used to indicate that the model was a subsequent version or destined to races. The Dialfa was characterized by its six-cylinder engine, which would not be used again on a Lancia for decades as performance by the four-cylinder was only slightly inferior. The desire to build excellent touring automobiles for the most demanding and wealthy clients forced Vincenzo Lancia to make a decision that perplexed many. He retired from racing and prohibited any official Lancia cars from participating in races. This was the same man who, when he was with Fiat, always won and who also did very well with his own cars. However, private individuals kept up the fame with victories that continued elevating the brand's reputation. Lancia presented the Beta, Gamma and Delta models, the sports models Didelta and Epsilon, Eta and Theta and the Zeta truck (which was also used in the military) before the start of World War I. These vehicles were equipped with many peculiarities and innovative features, which at times were even revolutionary. For example, the refined Theta was the first car in the world with a complete electrical system and metal wheels or spokes (rather than wooden). The Gamma was fast considering its weight, with a top speed of 68 mph (110 km/h), and was the best-selling model in this initial series (258 units were sold in 1910 alone). The 1911 Delta is remembered for being the first model manufactured in the large new Turinese factory at Via Monginevro (the factory was active until 1962, when the current one in Chiasso was opened), for its excellent brakes and high speeds (71 mph/115 km/h), which led to its sports version (Didelta).

52-53 Vincenzo Lancia behind the wheel of a Fiat 50 HP at the third running of the Targa Florio. Itt was held on 18 May 1908 at the Sicilian race on the Madonie Circuit and Lancia finished second.

53 An elegant Lancia Gamma 20 HP. It made its debut in 1911 and succeeded the 15-20 HP as the company's standard. A new, evolved and improved model was released every year.

54 top right *The 1913 Alfa 40-60 was a sporty thoroughbred with a six-cylinder, 6.1L (6082 cc), 70 hp engine that reached 75 mph (120 km/h). Twenty-seven units were manufactured and sold immediately. Two years later, it was the turn of the Corsa version, which made its debut at the Parma-Poggo Bercelo uphill race with Campari and Franchini coming in first and second in their category.*

54 top left *This 1910 24 HP was the first Alfa. It was equipped with a four-cylinder 4.1L (4084 cc), 42 HP engine, which was also used on the airplane that took flight in the skies of Milan in September of the same year to demonstrate this good engine and vehicle. It was a truly successful advertising stunt.*

Anonima Lombarda Fabbrica Automobile (Alfa) officially started its engines on June 24, 1910, even though activities had started the year before when a group of Lombard financial backers took over the Milanese plants of Darracq Italiana in Portello and restarted production with 500,000 Lira in capital. The first model, designed by surveyor Giuseppe Merosi – a pioneer of the engine with valves positioned in a 90° V, a configuration that would later become a classic on Italian engines – was created even before the company's official establishment. In fact it was January 1, 1910 when the 24 HP made its debut together with the new trademark, a *Biscione (serpent)* and red cross on a white background, symbolizing the Lombard capital. The vehicle stood out for its excellent road performance in terms of road-holding and speed, features it would always retain. A 40 hp, four-cylinder, inline, 4.1L (4084 cc) engine and variable speed depending on the series (A, B, C or D) could achieve 62-65 mph (100-105 km/h). The vehicle's success was also the result of the excellent and original publicity generated by the 24 HP engine. The engine was used in an airplane that flew over Milan as a demonstration of the project's effectiveness. In the meantime, the 20-30 HP, an updated version of the 24 HP with 49 hp, was created, and 680 units had been manufactured by 1920. They were used for multiple purposes, including a colonial version and a basic version used as work vehicles and as ambulances. The 40-60 HP was also created, with its corresponding Corsa version to increase the offer upwards. It was equipped with a 70-82 hp, six-cylinder, 6.1L (6082 cc) engine that reached a maximum speed of between 78 and 93 mph (125-150 km/h). It was a success, with the 25 units manufactured being sold immediately. But this vehicle made another mark in the history of the automobile, and not only for Alfa. Based on this chassis, Milanese Count Ricotti ordered a closed, tear-shaped body from Castagna with round, porthole-shaped windows. This vehicle, created in collaboration with Merosi, was the Siluro Ricotti and it represented greatness and the first aerodynamic exercise applied to an automobile. With this shape, the torpedo reached 86 mph (139 km/h), while racing models reached 93 mph (150 km/h). Strictly in terms of appearance, this 1914 model can also be considered as the forerunner of the modern minivan, as it was built in an era when unibody construction was still unfamiliar. Certainly, these vehicles were not known for their practicality or modularity; the driver's seat was in the middle of the vehicle and it was not intended to carry a lot of people.

In 1915 the company was first sold to Banca di Sconto, which in turn sold it to Neapolitan engineer Nicola Romeo. He took over the plants in Portello and converted them for wartime production. In 1918, Alfa became Società Anonima Ingegner Nicola Romeo & C., which took over Officine Meccaniche in Saronno, Officine Meccaniche Tabanelli in Rome and the Officine Ferroviarie Meridionali in Naples. The company's purpose was to manufacture automobiles, but also other machines (mining, chemical and farm-related) in addition to aero and locomotive engines. The intention to diversify was so clear that during the war production of automobiles virtually ceased because the plants were used to manufacture heavy means and aero engines. Reconversion was difficult but successful and, starting in 1919, the vehicles leaving the Milanese factory bore the trademark with its new name, Alfa-Romeo Milano.

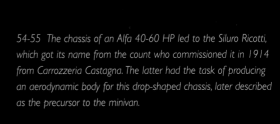

54-55 The chassis of an Alfa 40-60 HP led to the Siluro Ricotti, which got its name from the count who commissioned it in 1914 from Carrozzeria Castagna. The latter had the task of producing an aerodynamic body for this drop-shaped chassis, later described as the precursor to the minivan.

The voice of speed: the first races

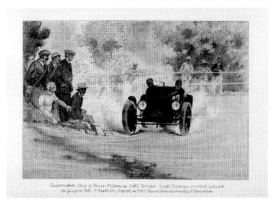

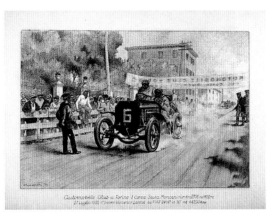

Cars mean racing. It is true that a vehicle is required in order to race, but it must be noted that races were the driving force behind the development of the car from all perspectives including mechanics, reliability, distribution, marketing and emotion. In this phase, if a manufacturer wanted to publicize an automobile, it took it to a competition or race to demonstrate the reliability of the project, the vehicle's solidity and its ability to go fast. And if all this happened, not only was it a public success but it also led to sales. This is what happened with Alfa or SPA, which was even assigned with a war job order by the Russian Minister of War as a result of the impressive performance by the Itala in 1908. It was driven by Ruggerone from Turin to St. Petersburg without any assistance. Then it participated in the St. Petersburg-Moscow race, where it came in second, and finally returned to Turin.

The call for speed is a challenge that mankind pursues and competes with until reaching, setting and even exceeding limits, resulting in imaginable consequences. The races of today and yesterday have been an extraordinary training ground on which to experiment all those devices that have then been transferred to everyday models or, as they were called back then, touring models. In the beginning, car races were held on roads between two towns and were to be run in the shortest time possible at the best average speed. These races were originally a few dozen miles and, as the reliability of the vehicles increased, they became much longer until they reached tens of thousands of miles, with some races lasting months.

Participants generally had large sums of money because taking part in them meant sustaining considerable costs for the vehicle, assistance and repairs. However, these wealthy individuals gladly sustained the costs because they appeased passions, evoked liberty and were elitist.

The first regulated race in the world took place in France, the Paris-Rouen held on July 22, 1894. Of the 21 vehicles at the starting line, 19 finished the race, and the winner was Georges Lemaitre in a Peugeot (the cars were judged on their handling and safety capacities, not the speed; in fact Lemaitre arrived second). The first Italian race, the Turin-Asti-Turin, was held the following year, on May 18, 1895. Five teams challenged each other along these 58 miles (93 kilometers), with Simone Federmann the winner racing a Daimler, followed by Giovanni Battista Ceirano on an engine-powered bicycle. Ceirano was an example of the many individuals and manufacturers who personally took part in races in order to understand how to build their models. Vincenzo Lancia, Ettore Bugatti, Oreste Fraschini and Carlo Maserati all did the same. At the same time, the development of races created the profession of the race-car driver, individuals who truly risked their life by racing cars and pushing their vehicle to new limits, often without living to tell the tale. In 1897 came the 21 mile (34 kilometer) Arona-Stresa-Arona race. The winner

was Giuseppe Cobianchi on a Benz, with an average speed of almost 14 mph (22 km/h), followed by Oreste Fraschini, also on a Benz. This race had a grand atmosphere, with people crowded along the route, country gentlemen running with their ladies to see, and perhaps later order, one of the vehicles as they darted by at speeds that were unthinkable for the time. The unwinding of the race for the drivers was often a true *via crucis*.

The roads were not paved, flat tires were a necessary evil and repairs were common for the mechanic who always accompanied the driver. Wheels were originally full rubber treads mounted on wooden rims with metal reinforcements. Tires with an independent air chamber covered with tire fabric anchored to the rim with two metal rings were invented by the Michelin brothers, who mounted them for the first time on a Peugeot Éclair at the Paris-Bordeaux-Paris race in 1895.

There was no comparison with the time required to restore the old flat tires, and even if the French vehicle in this race had to stop dozens of times for repairs, it would still cross the finishing line first. This was the beginning of tires as we know them today.

These races got underway in Italy with the aforementioned Turin-Asti-Turin race, and were soon being held everywhere. In 1901 the Automobile Tour of Italy, organized by the Italian Touring Club and sponsored by the *Corriere della Sera* newspaper, included several stages, each thousands of miles (or kilometers) long.

Participants could choose between the Turin-Rome-Milan route (1020 miles or 1642 km), Florence-Rome-Milan (684 miles or 1101 km) or Naples-Rome-Milan (665 miles or 1071 km).

This true marathon along the peninsula consolidated the concept of the automobile and of the race, which ran through cities and towns that prepared worthy welcomes for the passing teams, transformed the event into a celebration and included improving roads for the teams who drove increasingly reliable and high-performing vehicles.

The Automobile Tour of Italy accelerated the proliferation of races and witnessed an increasing number of participating racing drivers and vehicles. Coppa della Consuma, Circuito di Brescia, Circuito del Mugello, Milan-Sanremo, Parma-Poggio Berceto and Susa-Moncenisio were just a few of the races held between 1902 and the beginning of World War I.

57 *Team Faroun and Rezaire Nanddin in a Turinese race in 1900. Car racing was just beginning and was attracting competitors from all around the world, despite the dirt roads.*

58 Felice Nazzaro in a Fiat
28-40 HP in Petralia Sottana
during the 1907 Targa Florio.
He won the 276-mile (446
km) race in eight hours, 17
minutes and 36 seconds,
leaving second place to
Vincenzo Lancia (who also
drove a 28-40 HP).

58-59 Jean Porporato crossing
the finish line at the 1908
Targa Florio. He placed fourth
on a Berliet, a vehicle that got
its name from Marius Berliet, a
self-taught mechanic from Lyon
(France) who started building in
his automobile workshop in
1894. First place went to
Trucco on an Isotta Fraschini.

In 1906-1907 two events proudly flew the Italian flag in the racing world, the Targa Florio and the exhausting Paris-Beijing long-distance car rally, won by an Itala driven by an Italian team.

The first race was due to the desire, tenacity and inventiveness of Vincenzo Florio, the son of a rich family of merchants who also owned a large merchant fleet. Cars were Florio's passion, and he wanted to organize a large automobile race in his beloved Sicily. It was not a simple feat, considering that roads on the western part of the island were not great for a car race and many areas – especially in the hinterlands and the remote country-side – were ruled by bandits and brigands. Florio didn't give up, however, and after having organized the Coppa Florio in Brescia in 1905, he achieved his goal.

The Targa Florio officially started on May 6, 1906 with 10 teams ready to be challenged by an endurance race unwinding along 92 miles (148 km) up and down the Madonne hills. The race immediately met with international success. Alessandro Cagno on an Itala 115 HP came in first place and the Targa Florio, together with the subsequent Mille Miglia race, justifiably placed Italy in the exclusive circle of motor racing.

A little over a year later, Italy and the Itala were
once again in the spotlight. June 10 was the start of
the Paris-Beijing rally over an exhausting 9942 mile
(16,000-km) course. The starting line was in the
Chinese capital and of the 25 teams that registered
in January (after the Parisian newspaper *Le Matin*
proposed the challenge), only five showed up. One
of these was an Italian team on an Itala 35-45 HP
comprising Prince Scipione Borghese (Senator of
the Kingdom, great sportsman and man of motors),
mechanic Ettore Guizzardi from Emilia and Luigi
Barzini, a reporter for the *Corriere della Sera* and the
Daily Telegraph, who for the most part of the rally
had to sit on the floor of the vehicle, which only had

two seats. This did not keep him from sending his
dispatches to the newspapers via telegraph (when
he could find the facilities), describing this fascinating
race in which they almost immediately took the
lead. This was mostly thanks to Borghese, who had
trained himself and his Itala so well that during the
rally he took advantage of his enormous advantage
over the competition to make a 621 mile (1000 km)
detour in order to participate in a dance organized
in his honor by the Tsar of Russia (his distant
cousin). These three Italians – four if you include the
Itala itself – arrived victorious in Paris on August 10
to be welcomed by a jubilant crowd and admired
for their heroic enterprise.

62-63 A view of the Paris-Beijing race, the first long-distance car race in the history of the automobile, and the victorious Itala 35-45 HP being towed for repairs mechanic Ettore Guizzardi along a short section of the 9942 miles (16,000 km) driven in over two months.

63 top A break during the 1907 Paris-Beijing race. The Itala 35-45 HP is being checked by Prince Scipione Borghese (right) and by mechanic Ettore Guizzardi. The team also included journalist Luigi Barzini, who sent out telegraph dispatches (when he could find one) on the race.

63 bottom Ettore Guizzardi, the mechanic for Prince Scipione Borghese and the Itala 35-45 HP team that won the Paris-Beijing race, is behind the wheel of the vehicle performing the last checks before the start of the long-distance car rally in the Chinese capital on June 10, 1907.

CHAPTER 2

The 1920s,
a unique decade

Between reconversion and the great crisis

65 *Fiat's futuristic 1928 poster by Giuseppe Riccobaldi del Bava was inspired by the access ramp to the Lingotto.*

66-67 *Felice Nazzaro behind the wheel of a Fiat 804 at the 1922 French Grand Prix in Strasburg. He was the first to cross the finish line.*

67 top *La Fongri produced motorcycles at the beginning of the twentieth century in addition to special projects such as this vehicle.*

Those automakers that made it to World War I but failed to expand their plants or standardize production as the automobile's industrial system demanded, were lifeless after the conflict and lacked the capital and ideas they needed to avoid being crushed by the competition. The Great War, just like World War II, led to natural selection. Only the strongest and most organized survived and were able to continue their journey and create a page in history. Another uncertainty was produc-

tion and machinery reconversion. Italian manufacturers, like those around the world, were further screened by the return to normality and changes in demand from bullets and heavy vehicles to cars used for civil purposes. Yet another painstaking reason was the Italian government's full or partial failure to make payments for the war job orders, which had been the only client during the war. Just when the economy was showing signs of recovery and the period of interrupted production and consumption due to high unemployment seemed over, the Wall Street crash of 1929 came along,

leading to a deep economic depression. Despite this disconcerting picture, which was tied both to a political crisis and deep-rooted nationalism that led to Fascism, Italy's automobile sector experienced a time of great prosperity. It offered great technological innovations on one hand and style and elegance on the other that was highly regarded and sought after around the world. The number of Italians behind the wheel multiplied along with the number of vehicles on the road, which increased from 24,000 vehicles in 1919 to in excess of 186,000 at the start of the 1930s. The first high-

way in the world, the Milano-Laghi, was inaugurated in 1923. The number of manufacturers slowly decreased, however. Those that continued included an evolving Fiat, which motorized Italy, Lancia, with its characteristically elegant, comfortable and innovative models, and Alfa Romeo, which stood out for its sportiness, allowing it to reap success in races and boast international admirers – including Henry Ford, who famously said, "When I see an Alfa Romeo go by, I tip my hat."

Companies like Ansaldo, Chiribiri, Diatto, and SCAT closed down while Bianchi, Isotta Fraschini and Itala experienced a period of crisis. A few new manufacturers were merely flashes in the pan, such as Ansaldo, an engineering complex and one of the most important corporate structures in Italy, which produced everything from manufacturing airplanes and ships to railway material. In 1919, it began manufacturing automobiles with the necessary quantity and quality to ensure longevity, but it experienced economic misfortunes and a financial crisis, and the final blow arrived with the great depression. Another example was Nazzaro. In 1919, racing driver Felice Nazzaro again attempted to transfer the experience and notoriety he had gained from racing into success as an automaker, but just as had happened the first time (from 1912 to 1916), he closed down after four years and returned to Fiat as a test and racing driver. One company that had a slightly longer history was Temperino, named after two brothers. In 1919 the brothers, who were first bicycle and later motorcycle manufacturers, began producing a small vehicle based on a project developed before the war. It was the 8-10 HP with various bodies, from an open sports car to a two-seater and van with a moderate-sized engine. It was successful, thanks to race victories and, as a result, the Temperino brothers negotiated production agreements with Opessi (a Turinese weights and measures factory) and with Farina, who produced the bodies Opessi had already been called to participate in the birth of Fi-

at). Temperino also succeeded in its export endeavors and opened an English branch, but it was not able to survive the economic crisis and closed down in 1925. Saba, a small Milanese company, operated from 1923 to 1928 and stood out for the production of its Stelvio model, which was the first Italian 4x4 and was also equipped with four-wheel steering. Economic problems prevented it from being marketed.

67 center The Diatto Tipo 20 manufactured from 1920 to 1923 was an elegant, torpedo-shaped, two-tone vehicle equipped with a 2.0L (1996 cc), 40 hp engine (increased to 75 hp in the S Spinta version).

67 bottom The 1923 Ansaldo 4C was the Turinese manufacturer's most popular model and was also available in an S (Spinto) version used by drivers like Tazio Nuvolari to gain experience.

68 During the Great War manufacturing focused on ships, airplanes, weapons and railway material, but reconversion also led to the production of automobiles: The first model to leave the Ansaldo factory was the 4A.

68-69 Several solderers at work with sheet metal in the Ansaldo factory. This was one of the leading Italian companies during WWI and employed 80,000 workers in 30 plants.

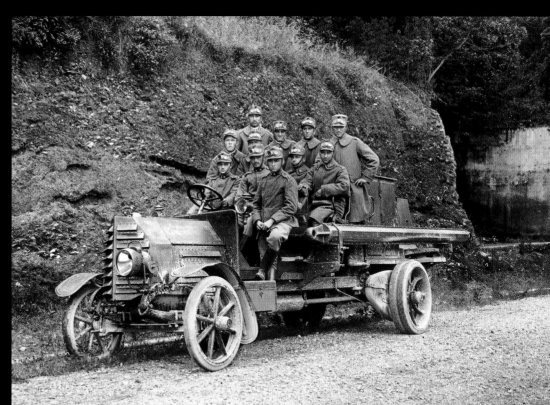

The history of the Maserati brothers started in 1887, the year Carlo was born. The first of six sons, he took his first steps in the field of mechanics at the age of 17 by designing and creating a bicycle motor. He later worked for Fiat, Isotta Fraschini, Bianchi and Junior. He died at the age of 29, but was enough of an example for brothers Alfieri, Ettore and Ernesto, who established SA Officine Alfieri Maserati in Bologna in 1914. The company specialized in developing Isotta Fraschini vehicles and made its debut in 1926 with the T26, the first vehicle bearing the trademark of the *Tridente* (the three-pronged fork). The *Tridente* automaker was the only new entry to the group of existing manufacturers during the decade, which to this day symbolizes performance and racing. After the war, Alfieri proved himself as a racing driver and also started collaborating with Diatto by designing and driving its race cars. Disqualification during a race for using a 3.0L (3000 cc) rather than a 2.0L (2000 cc) engine brought an end to his collaboration with the Turinese brand (which closed down in 1928) and allowed him to completely devote himself to the production of vehicles. His pro-

found commitment led to the creation of their first vehicle, the Tipo 26, designed by younger brother Mario, which Alfieri himself drove to win his category in the Targa Florio. Success in the most demanding and famous race provided a resounding boost for Maserati, which became the great new Italian hope for racing success. Even when it didn't officially participate in competitions, private individuals kept the *Tridente*'s flag flying high. The 1929 V4 with a 16-cylinder engine allowed the company to expand, thanks to the six-mile (10 km) category C world speed record of 153 mph (246 km/h) set by Baconin Borzacchini at the Italian Grand Prix.

Some manufacturers continued and some

closed down, while others, such as OM, SPA and Scat-Ceirano, were taken over by Fiat. Officine Meccaniche (OM) was a company from Brescia created in 1918. It manufactured the S305, which was still on the drawing table of another local manufactured, Zust, when it was taken over by OM. Its most representational model was certainly the 1934 665, which was also known as the Superba, due to its sportiness and the elegant body that car designers such as Castagna made for it. The 665 also gained recognition at the first edition of the Mille Miglia in 1927, when it grabbed first, second, and third places. It reduced its car production when it became part of Fiat in 1933 and finally stopped altogether in 1937, when it only manufactured commercial vehicles and was taken over by Iveco. Turinese SPA survived the war without much difficulty and combined its profitable and consolidated production of trucks with that of touring automobiles like the Tipo 24 and 25, which carved out their own niche in the market. This share of the market interested Fiat, who bought the company and its plants employing over 700 workers in 1926. It refocused the company's production back towards trucks and military vehicles and thus become the leading supplier for the Italian armed forces. Finally, the crisis in 1929 clipped the wings of Scat-Ceirano despite the positive sale of the 150, its leading model. Here too, automobile production was stopped and the plants started being used for industrial vehicles.

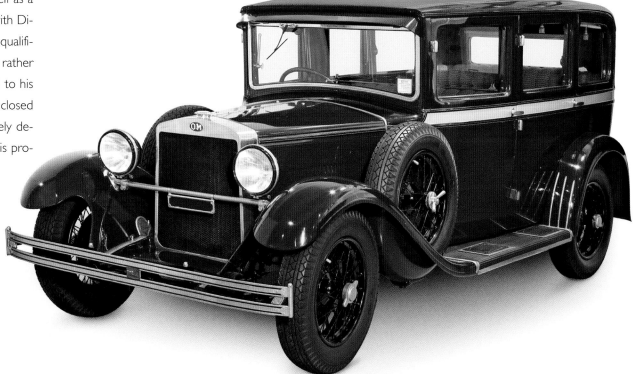

Isotta Fraschini's Tipo 8, the masterpiece envied by the world

This was the best Italian car in the world in a decade lacking economic and political certainties. Once again, this demonstrated the ability of Italians to assert themselves and show their backbone during the toughest of times. The architects of the Isotta Fraschini Tipo 8's success were Ludovico Mazzotti and Giustino Cattaneo. The former became a partner in the Milanese automaker during its financial restructuring, which required new capital due to late payments for war supplies by the government. This new structure also outlined the brand's new strategy, which aimed at a very high, international target – the same target that was usually left unharmed by crises or negative circumstances. Then the Tipo 8 was born and Cattaneo came into play because he produced it, resulting in a *laurea honoris* in engineering that confirmed the project's excellence. Paradoxically, Cattaneo had it easy. It is true he had to invent a vehicle that helped the brand recover, brought it

prestige and was able to compete internationally with Hispano-Suiza, Rolls-Royce, Mercedes-Benz and Duesemberg, but he had unlimited resources and no orders to make affordable vehicles, which allowed him to develop the best technology and create the most elegant vehicle possible. For the first time anywhere, the Tipo 8 mounted a mass-produced eight-cylinder, inline engine with a displacement whose various evolutions (8A, 8AS, 8ASS, 8B) from 1919 to 1931 increased from 5.9L (5901 cc) to 7.4L (7370 cc), 80-135 hp, 62-87 mph (100-140 km/h) with consumption equal to two to three miles (3.4-5 km) with 0.22 gallons (1 L). Furthermore, its production elegance and the quest for perfection and attention to every last detail made this vehicle an object of desire in which the best car designers (Castagna and Touring firstly) could indulge their whims, thanks to clients who ordered it and spared no expense to have it personalized. Then there was the price, another element that contributed to making it unique and desired by wealthy and famous individuals all over the world. The Tipo 8 and its various versions ended up costing 150,000 Lira, plus at least an additional 30,000 Lira for the bodywork. Compare this with the Balilla, which cost 10,800 Lira. The United States was the main market for the most sought after vehicle at that time. Hollywood movie stars and magnates were the most loyal clients, in addition to royalty and nobles from all around the globe. Some of the most famous examples are Castagna's 8A used in the mammoth production *Il viale del tramonto*, Touring's Flying Star on an 8B chassis that won the 1931 Concours d'Elegance in Genoa, an aerodynamic coupe by Viotti for Victor Emanuel III, and two units for Rudolf Valentino by American car designer Fleetwood.

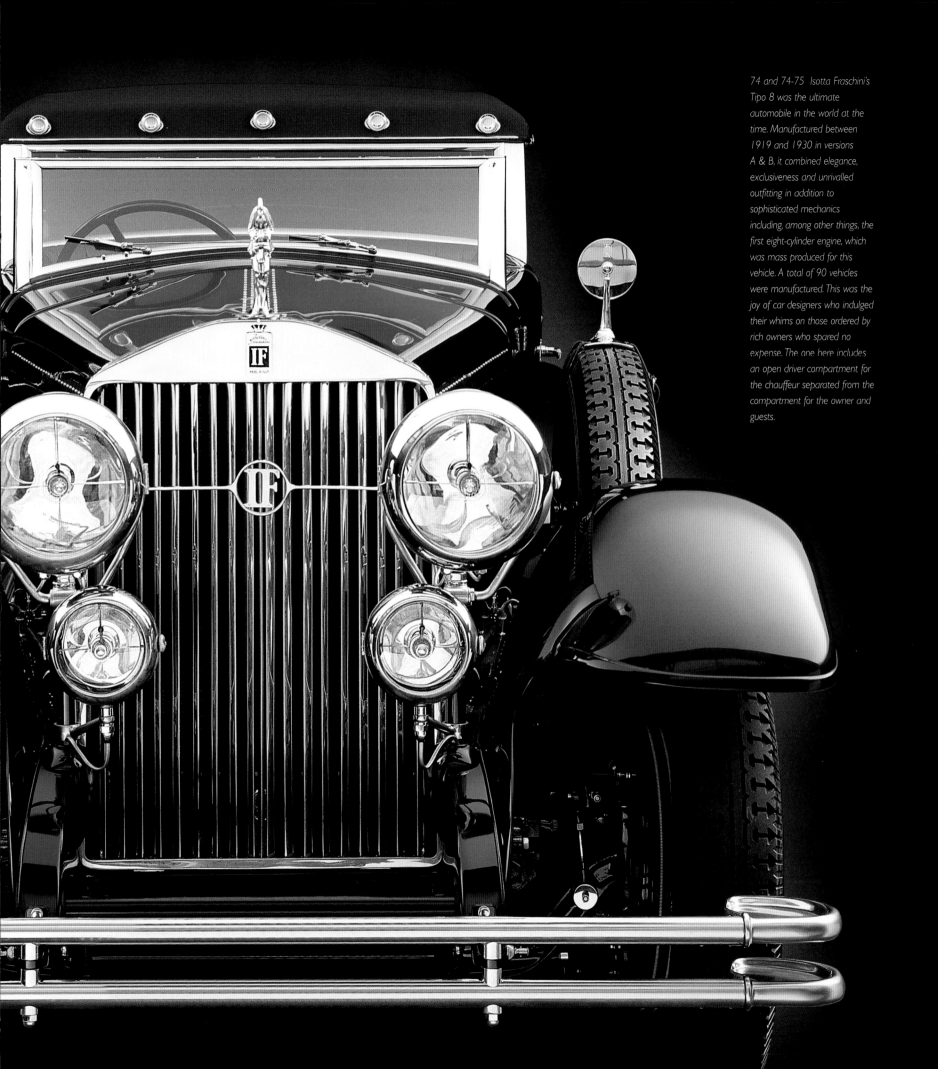

74 and 74-75 Isotta Fraschini's Tipo 8 was the ultimate automobile in the world at the time. Manufactured between 1919 and 1930 in versions A & B, it combined elegance, exclusiveness and unrivalled outfitting in addition to sophisticated mechanics including, among other things, the first eight-cylinder engine, which was mass produced for this vehicle. A total of 90 vehicles were manufactured. This was the joy of car designers who indulged their whims on those ordered by rich owners who spared no expense. The one here includes an open driver compartment for the chauffeur separated from the compartment for the owner and guests.

Lancia Lambda: the new symbol of Italian excellence

Revolutionary. Even the most cursory comparison of this vehicle's features with those offered by the market at the time makes it clear that this was a car that marked a change. Supporting bodywork, front suspensions with independent wheels, a transmission tunnel on the floor in addition to a narrow-angle V, four-cylinder engine, chassis, streamlined profile with an integrated trunk following the shape of the car, and reduced height (the thickness of the frame was no longer necessary) providing brilliant performance and extreme ease of handling. This was the Lancia Lambda's calling card, the maximum expression of Vincenzo Lancia's genius, which seemed inspired by a naval vessel and resulted in the vehicle's shapes and technical solutions. The presentation of the prototype at the London and Paris Auto Shows in 1922 was greeted with jubilation and Lancia personally brought the vehicle back to Turin accompanied by his wife (they had just returned from their honeymoon). Vincenzo was now famous world-wide and had already sold over

5000 cars – even the great writer, Gabriele d'Annunzio traveled in one of his vehicles. Giacomo Puccini, the operatic composer and a great automobile enthusiast, ordered a vehicle from Lancia that was able to navigate even the most difficult of terrains. After just a few months of waiting, he received what could be considered the first Italian off-road vehicle with a reinforced chassis and studded wheels. The maestro's satisfaction was so great that he purchased a Trikappa and a Lambda. This was that same Lambda that took him on his last trip, on November 4, 1924, to the station in Pisa where he took a train for Brussels to undergo what turned out to be a fatal operation. The Lambda was the vehicle that immortalized Lancia. It first went on sale in 1923, by which time there was already a very long waiting list. A total of nine series were manufactured until 1931, a total of 13,000 vehicles. The first five versions had slight modifications and improvements, and later changes included a new gearbox, increased horsepower (from 2.1L or 2120 cc and

76 top Villa Puccini at Torre del Lago in the Italian province of Lucca at the beginning of the twentieth century. Giacomo Puccini, accompanied by his wife Elvira, is in the car on the left; his son is in the other car.

76 bottom and 77 bottom The Lancia Lambda made its debut in 1922 at the Paris Auto Show and was an

unprecedented success. This vehicle revolutionized automobile manufacturing rules and had innovations that made a permanent mark in the history of four–door vehicles. The most important innovations involved the bodywork acting as a supporting structure and front suspensions with independent wheels.

49 hp to 2.6L or 2568 cc and 69 hp) and other alterations related to appearance and mechanics. They also all had different bodies, thanks to a choice of chassis with different wheelbases, and were available at prices starting from 43,000 Lira.

The Lambda was the perfect example of how technology and design could be combined and was the best expression of the so-called classic car developed during this decade. In fact, some time between 1929 and 1930, the engine hood was integrated with the driver and passenger compartment to form a single body from the radiator to the windshield. The vehicle's overall width did not change between the underhood and passenger area as the side, rear and top portions intersected and the choice of convex or straight shapes depended on the type of vehicle. The fenders, however, remained an autonomous appendage for the time being. The height and external size generally depended on the type of automobile, which in this case referred to the categories of the time, ranging from the

sedan and convertible to the sports coupe. All of this despite the presence of numerous coachbuilders and clients ordering vehicles based on their own tastes. In terms of the Lancia, it is understandable how this automaker was experiencing a moment of glory, but not only thanks to the Lambda. It came out of the war and rightly focused on manufacturing industrial vehicles by exploiting the engines assembled on the Kappa and Dikappa. During the war it had patented the narrow-V engine used in Caproni fighter planes. The requirement in this case was to have a high-powered engine with a very small overall size. The decade also witnessed the debut of the Kappa (1919), the first car in the world to have an adjustable steering column, as well as its variants, the Dikappa (1921) and the Trikappa (1922, with a V8 engine), and the flagship Dilambda (1929), which replaced the Trikappa. The Dilambda was presented at the New York Auto Show in order to take a peak at the American market, where Lancia had an excellent reputation.

77 top Giacomo Puccini was an automobile enthusiast, especially of Lancias. In this picture from the early 1900s, he is behind the wheel sitting beside Gabriele d'Annunzio and Marco Praga is behind to the left.

78-79 The eighth series of the Lancia Lambda made its debut in 1928. It was the second-last series of this very successful vehicle, which was the masterpiece of eclectic personality and avant-gardist

Vincenzo Lancia. The revolution of the Lambda was the result of his observations during a cruise, when he noticed the ship's structure comprised the keel and hull. This was also the most popular generation in terms of sales (3903 were sold out of a total 13,003 manufactured between 1922-1931). The car was characterized by the umpteenth increase in power to the four-cylinder V engine, which was raised from 2.4L (2370 cc) to 2.6L (2568 cc) and reached 69 hp.

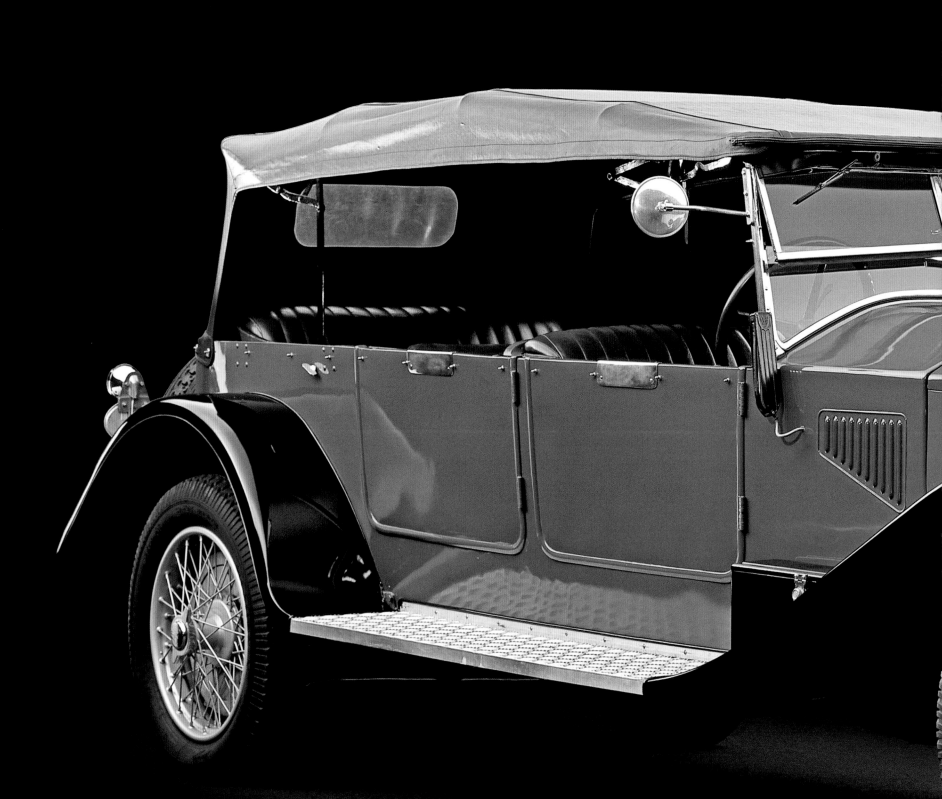

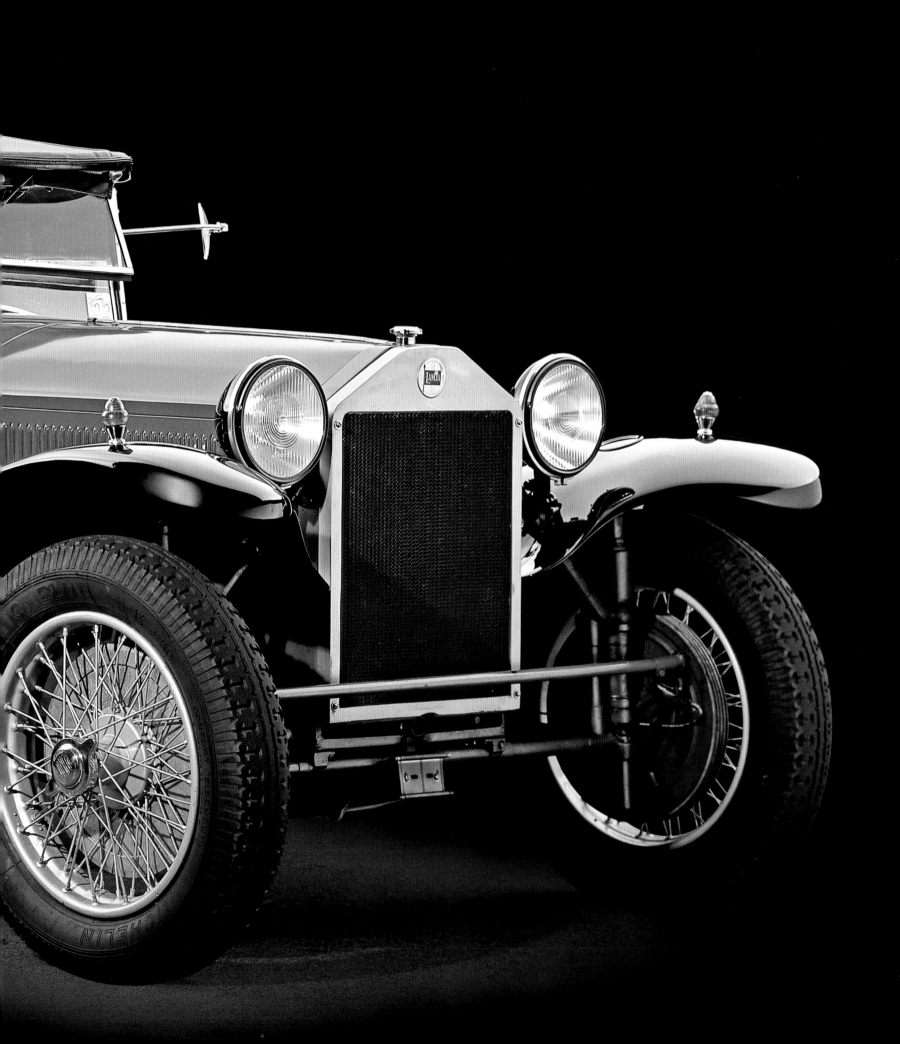

Fiat continued to motorize Italy

Fiat certainly had no problems with reconversion. In any event, the economic crisis of 1929 did not threaten the life of this Italian giant, largely because of all its acquisitions and the crises that other organizations, such as Ansaldo, were experiencing. Fiat became the leader of the Italian industry and was increasingly tied to the vicissitudes and political life of Italy. Despite this, it was a difficult decade due to the social, economic and automotive transformations. In 1926 Giovanni Agnelli (who had been chairman of Fiat since 1920) asked Gabriele d'Annunzio to settle the controversy concerning the gender of the automobile, considering that in Italian the word was masculine, but was feminine in French. The term, which is of French origin, was originally an adjective, as in the expression *voiture automobile*. In 1890 it first became a noun and then, after fiery debate, a feminine noun. Even with d'Annunzio's input, the word automobile remained feminine.

Fiat coped with its varying crises. Logical price curbing led to reductions in personnel and wages, in turn causing trade union unrest that took a toll on production. Foreign orders were received but it was difficult to dispatch them. In terms of international expansion, Fiat Polski was established in 1921 to manufacture cars and trucks under license in Russia.

In 1927, IFI (Istituto Finanziario Industriale) was established to coordinate all of the company's interests and acquisitions, even in non-automobile sectors. There was also the acquisition of Italian newspaper *La Stampa* (1926) and its dominant presence in the Italian national railways, and in the shipbuilding and aviation industries and aviation. As for production, Fiat opened the Lingotto factory (in excess of 1.615 million sq ft or 150,000 sq m) in 1923 and the first car to be mass produced in this cutting-edge plant was the 509.

Ninety thousand units rolled off the assembly lines, the huge distribution owing to the good price-outfitting ratio (even though the 509 was not as reliable as the 501) and also because, for the first time ever, it could be purchased on an installment plan through the newly established Sava company.

80 and 80-81 The new Fiat Lingotto factory in Turin was designed by engineer Giacome Mattè Trucco. It also included a vast oval area on the roof, where vehicles – especially race cars – could be tested. The Lingotto was inaugurated in May 1923 and was equipped with the most modern production machinery. The vehicle intended for mass production in the plant was the 509.

81 bottom left Gigantic presses occupy the Fiat factory in Turin where workers press sheet metal, which is later painted.

81 bottom right Phase of the Fiat 501 assembly line in 1923: engine-steering group assembled in the Fiat factory in Turin.

The solid and successful 501 was a post-war vehicle with the task of continuing the mass-motorization of the country. It was reliable, mid-size, had low operating costs and with an untiring and simple four-cylinder, 1.5L (1460 cc) engine, it was used in the most demanding ways without any problems, all of which made it highly regarded abroad. The 501 was also Fiat's first model prepared by Siata (Società Italiana Trasformazioni Applicazioni Automobilistiche), founded in 1926 by racing driver Giorgio Ambrosiani, the headquarters of which were just a short distance from Fiat's main factory. Transformations were concretized in the sports version of production models, which were equipped with considerable horsepower and were quite successful in competitions. The 505 and its evolutions, the 507 and 510 and later the 512, fell into the mid-to-high categories, the latter being exported mainly to Great Britain and Australia. The true flagship was the 519, introduced in 1923, which featured a sporty six-cylinder engine, great elegance and outfitting. Today it would be the classic official car, updated with the 1928 model 525, which was equipped with a long wheelbase able to transport up to seven passengers (one was donated to Pope Pius X). The 120 model was equipped with a six–cylinder engine, brought fortune to the 520 and inaugurated a generation of engines with different sized cylinders that could be mounted on several vehicles.

82 Plinio Codognato designed this advertising poster for the Fiat 514 in 1929: Commanding and important graphic characterization was dedicated to the vehicle's numeric name.

its four years of production. Available in sedan, torpedo-shaped, convertible and coupe versions, it was a hit with the public thanks to its excellent reliability and great attention to detail.

83 The 1929 Fiat 509 Spider was one of versions of this small vehicle and the first to be manufactured in the Turinese manufacturer's new factory, the Lingotto. Over 90,000 units were sold during

84 and 85 The 1926 Fiat 512 reaped the rewards sown by the 1919 Fiat 510, Fiat's first luxury car after the war, and stood out for the improvements made to the suspensions and brake system.

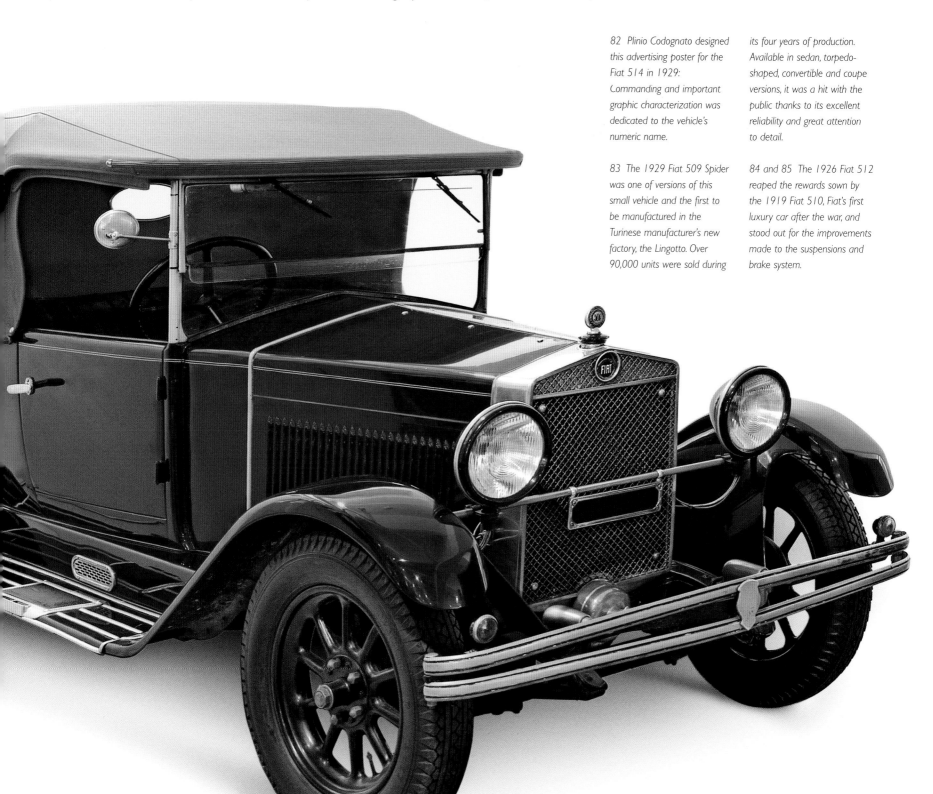

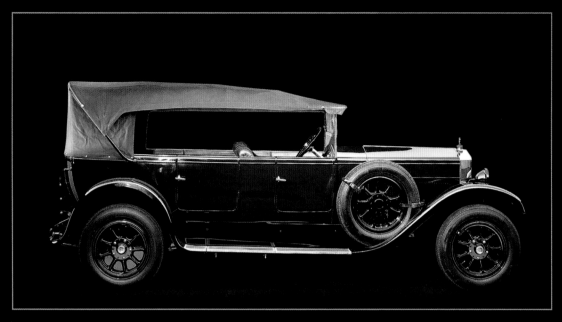

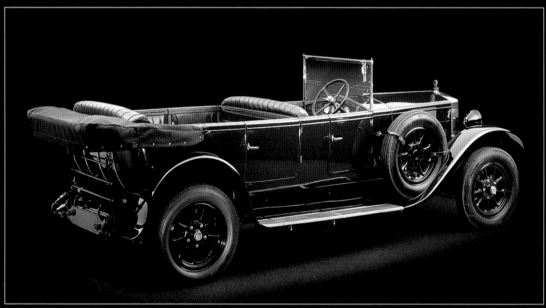

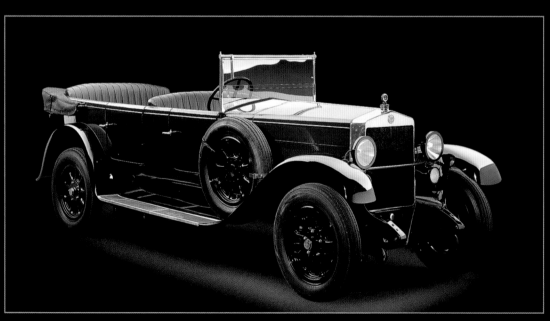

Alfa Romeo's enchanting 6C 1750

While the 1920s was a magical decade for racing, it was a little less so for mass production, but this was certainly not due to the quality of the products, which was indisputable. Alfa Romeo vehicles were sought after and had racing in their DNA, so it was natural they were not able to match Fiat, which in 1926 manufactured somewhere in the neighborhood of 37,000 vehicles, compared with the 1000 or so of the Portello automaker. But the crisis in 1929 was a terrible enemy and steps had to be taken against it. The policy of downsizing (which did not appeal to Romeo, who consequently left the chairmanship) and the direction of production towards more commercial, lighter and less powerful models without overlooking its sporty philosophy and sophisticated mechanics, led to the 6C 1500 and 6C 1750 models, designed by Vittorio Jano, in 1927 and

1929 respectively, and the stabilization of the company's economic situation. Jano was born in Turin in 1891 and brought fortune to automakers, initially Fiat but especially to Alfa Romeo, in the sports sector for almost a half a century. Gianni Lancia also wanted Jano to design the Formula One D50 and he collaborated intensely with Enzo Ferrari. The 6C 1750 (the developed evolution of the 6C 1500) became and remained one of the symbolic models of this Milanese brand. During its four years in production (1929-1933) 2259 units were manufactured, which was a very high number for Alfa Romeo. Powerful, first-class mechanics and sophisticated outfitting dominated competitions for two years, resulting in great benefits in terms of sales. The Turismo, Sport and Super Sport versions, with various bodies ranging from the open sports car to the sedan and torpedo, climaxed with the Gran Sport, which was requested world-wide and won races everywhere. The Gran Sport Compressore was the last in the dynasty of this exceptional vehicle.

Preceding these vehicles, however, was the 1029 20-30 ES Sport. It was the first post-war model and a descendent of the veteran 20-30 HP, but had improved performance, a shorter wheelbase and a

newly designed radiator. Most of the units produced were used in competitions, a 20-30 ES Sport was the first official vehicle of Alfa Romeo racing driver Enzo Ferrari. Ferrari was born in Modena in February of 1898 and became one of the most famous of all Italians. In 1924 he was appointed *Cavaliere del lavoro* – an Italian honor awarded to important industrial figures – for his sporting achievements. In any event, Alfa and its car allowed Baroness Avanzo to win the Coppa delle Dame in Brescia in 1921. The 1921 RL and 1923 RM were designed to race, even if the bodywork of many chassis were fitted by Castagna, Sala and Zagato, giving life to marvelous, elegant vehicles with a unique sporty touch. The RL mounted the first engine produced by Alfa Romeo. It was a six-cylinder engine designed by Merosi with a single shaft in the Touring versions and a twin-shaft in the Sport version. This high performance vehicle was almost unbeatable in endurance, speed and uphill racing and it collected almost 100 touring class victories, thanks also to racing drivers of the caliber of Ascari and Ferrari. The RM was less fortunate. It mounted the same four- or six-cylinder engine, with the cubic volume reduced from 3.0L to 2.0L (3000 cc to 2000 cc). The clientele continued to favor the RL.

86 The King of Italy, Victor Emanuel III, on an Alfa Romeo RM with an extended wheelbase that allowed additional passengers to be seated in a third row.

87 This advertising poster best communicated the sporty elegance that characterized Alfa Romeo. The manufacturer won the 1925 World Championship with the P, giving the trademark its laurel.

CAMPIONE DEL MONDO

SOCIETÀ ANONIMA ITALIANA

Ing. NICOLA ROMEO & C.

MILANO

88-89 This 1925 Alfa Romeo RL was one of the greatest expressions of Vittorio Merosi's creative genius. This vehicle was created in 1921 out of respect for the new formula for international races. It was equipped with a 3.0 L, six-cylinder engine with a removable cylinder-head. It was Alfa Romeo's first monobloc and lent determination and performance to this vehicle manufactured in two versions: Normale 56 hp and Sport 71 hp. The Sport version had a shorter wheelbase allowing the Super Sport version to reach 83 hp. It was elusive in races and racing drivers the likes of Enzo Ferrari, Antonio Ascari and Gastone Brilli-Peri got carried away behind its wheel.

International races spoke Italian

The exceptional popularity of automobile races in all forms (track, endurance, uphill) and the power of Italian racing drivers and cars in races all over the world in this period were unrivalled right up until recent times. It may have been a reaction to the difficulties of the post-war period and the economic crisis at the end of the 20s – whatever the reason, the fact is the Italian flag flew on the highest spot on the podium many times.

The birth in 1922 of the Monza speedway, the

international temple for speed, and the Mille Miglia in 1927, the most beautiful race in the world along the 1600 km (1000 mile) Brescia-Rome-Brescia route, were the icing on the cake. The unfortunate death of Antonio Ascari in 1925 at the French Grand Prix should also be mentioned.

Alfa Romeo was exuberant and uncontainable. Its race division with Vittorio Jano and Enzo Ferrari (the Ferrari Team was started in 1929 and managed the Milanese automaker's racing team) brought about the creation of the P2, allowing Gastone Brilli-Peri to win the first World Championship on the Monza circuit in 1925. The RL dominated the touring car races and showed off in the first Mille Miglia once again with Brilli-Peri paired up with Presenti, and only a small breakdown spoiled otherwise excellent results. However, Campari's 6C 1500 won the 1928 Mille Miglia and the following year seven 6C 1750 making their sports debuts placed in the top 10.

In 1932 the 6C 1750 Compressore once again showed off by winning its category. As for Fiat, it won the Italian Grand Prix in 1923 with Carlo Salamano, after Pietro Bordino had recorded the best lap time at the same event two years earlier before being forced to pull out of the race due to mechanical problems. In 1928 the 509 came in first and second at the Monte Carlo rally. The 525S won the Coppa delle Alpi and actually led the way to the modified version 525SS.

Even if Lancia didn't officially participate, it gave its private drivers satisfaction. For example, the Lambda came in third and fourth at the first Mille Miglia in 1927 (winning with an OM) and third the following year. Even the majestic Isotta Fraschini managed well in road races, "French" Bugatti won the Italian Championship with the magnificent 35 in 1927, while Maserati – racing as Alfa Romeo – was simply ferocious.

In addition to the aforementioned victory in its category by the Tipo 26 at its sports debut in the

Targa Florio in 1926, it went on to win the Italiano Marche Championship the following year as well.

Alfieri Maserati's serious accident in 1927 on a Tipo 26B at the Coppa Messina should also be mentioned. Then in 1930, the V4, 16-cylinder won the Tripoli Grand Prix with Baconin Borzacchini, and three years later it was the turn of Tazio Nuvolari.

91 bottom The finish line at the 1922 Targa Florio. This well known Italian race – one of the most famous in the world, along with the Mille Miglia – took place in Sicily from 1906 to 1977 and was only temporarily discontinued during the two world wars.

92 This advertising poster for Fiat was dedicated to the races in the 1920s. It was created by well known artists who attested to the Italian manufacturer's success and supremacy in car racing at the time.

93 This racing vehicle is a Fiat SB4, better known as Mephistopheles in light of the resounding noise it made due to the absence of an exhaust pipe. Created to conquer speed records, it dates back to 1924 and was modified by Ernest Eldridge, who equipped it with a six-cylinder, 21.0L (21,000 cc), 320 hp aero-engine. The chassis was lengthened to give the engine the extra space it required. It established a new speed record in Arpajon (France) in July 1924 by reaching 143 mph (230 km/h).

CHAPTER 3

From the crisis
in 1929 to the war

Aerodynamics and
the motorization of the working-class

During the period between the Wall Street crash of 1929 and World War II, Italian automobile shapes took a new course. Developments in aerodynamics gave life to tapered and tear-shaped models with tilted windshields and radiators and lights increasingly integrated in the front end, while fenders were moved in closer to the body of the vehicle and running boards disappeared for good. Automobile production quantities seesawed and, consequently, so did sales.

make a tangible mark in history. Races were a formidable resounding vehicle for the four-wheelers – particularly the Mille Miglia.

Alfa Romeo's successes with models bearing the Milanese trademark were even able to seduce Mussolini (a great automobile enthusiast) and to persuade the average Italian, who loved and cars and invested them with values far beyond that of a simple means of transport. Individuals also had to consider the purchasing power of their wages, however, which generally did not allow them to buy the vehicles they wanted.

This did not prevent the spread of motorization, although it still was not something for the masses. Fascism contributed, through the construction of highways, to an increase in the number of vehicles in circulation.

In truth, the regime's intent was more than just making cars an item for the masses. Rather, it intended to demonstrate its ability to innovate and follow technological progress, allowing it to

For example, a worker in their mid 30s earned approximately 350 Lira per month, a blue-collar worker 250 Lira and a farmer less than 100 Lira. If a Fiat Topolino cost 8900 Lira, a Lancia Ardea 29,000 Lira and an Alfa Romeo 8C as much as 91,000 Lira, it is understandable that the car remained a dream for many and the bicycle continued to do the job (considering that one could be purchased for under 600 Lira).

94-95 Alfa Romeo participated in the 1936 Mille Miglia with its new 8C 2900 B and took first, second, and third places.

96-97 Prince Bira of Siam on a curve on the Brooklands Campbell Circuit in his 3.0 L (3000 cc), eight-cylinder Maserati during the Junior Car Club 200 Mile Race held on April 27, 1938.

96 bottom Tazio Nuvolari also helped develop the 1933 Maserati 8CM. It won the Belgian, Montenero and Nice Grands Prix with Mantovano behind the wheel and was a match for Mercedes and Auto Union.

97 A mechanic services and fine-tunes a 1938 Maserati 6CM.

These social conditions were confirmed by the sales figures. The record number of cars sold in 1929 (before the start of the depression) was 33,436 units and this number was not exceeded until 1937, when 34,208 units were sold. Sales improved the following year, reaching 38,675 units, a figure that was not bettered until 48,883 units were sold in 1949, by which time the war was a thing of the past and recovery was about to be become an economic boom. The number of vehicles in Italy at the end of the 1920s was one for every 250 people. The equivalent number in Great Britain was one for every 37 people, in France one to 40 and in the United States, an amaz-

ing rate of one car for every 10 people. Europe in general had fallen behind other regions, where high market volumes and extremely competitive prices had accelerated the development of the automobile and practices that are still in use today. This is where the first style centers were created and methods were invented to stimulate sales or change cars, such as previewing a new model through the use of concept cars or show cars. This was the so-called model year that in fact programmed a vehicle's lifecycle, leaving the scene to make room for another one that was restyled, and brand differentiation. Europe had set the pace but had now fallen behind. The war in-

terrupted the growth and the evolution of automobiles until the post-war period, when production lines were converted and started up again, beginning with projects from the 1930s, which led to the creation of models that, in some cases, remained in production for many decades. In Italy this was the case of the Fiat Topolino, which sold approximately 520,000 units between 1936 and 1955 in its various generations – A, B and C – and with Berlinetta, Giardiniera and Belvedere bodies. This was considerable volume for the Italian market, even if it was small compared to the multi-million sales of models such as the Citröen 2 CV or the Volkswagen Beetle.

98-99 The body of this 1937 Alfa Romeo 8C 2900B Spider is on a long-wheelbase chassis. Beautiful and successful, it was the car to beat at races thanks to its powerful mechanics (it was equipped with an eight-cylinder, 220 hp engine with two positive displacement compressors) and quality chassis.

99 top Il Duce, Benito Mussolini, visiting Rome in 1941 on the state version of the Alfa Romeo 6C 2300 manufactured on a chassis with an extended wheelbase that made it possible to seat up to six people.

The birth of the Fiat Balilla and Topolino

"Baptized with the prophetic name of the new Italian youth, the Balilla [the name also given to the members of the Italian Fascist Youth Movement aged 8-14] is an automobile that is finally making its way towards the people." This is how Benito Mussolini baptized the 508. It was one of Fiat's symbolic vehicles, as indicated by the periodical *Le vie d'Italia* when it was presented at the factory in Turin by Giovanni Agnelli. It was April 9, 1932 – three days before it

made its official debut at the Milan Auto Show. Certainly, the Balilla's price was not really suitable for the working class, but it was the least expensive at the time and represented Fiat's attempts to re-launch motorization that had been mortified by the recently ended crisis. At 10,800 Lira, which became 9,900 in the fall of the same year (payable in installments), the Balilla was certainly the most reasonably priced Fiat, and its successful sales were also due to its ease of handling and affordability. Easy to drive, even on winding roads, it had a compact 1.0L (995 cc), 20 hp engine that reached 53 mph (85 km/h), resulting in good performance, reduced consumption and simple maintenance. Furthermore, despite its compact size, it held up to four passengers without too much difficulty. After the Zero, Fiat once again confirmed its inclination towards small models for widespread distribution, a focus that is still visible with today's new Panda and 500 models. The Balilla was suitable for

everything and in May 1932, *Le vie d'Italia* perfectly described its mission (albeit in rather propagandistic tones): "Industrialists, merchants, shopkeepers and employees, doctors, accountants, lawyers, surveyors, entrepreneurs, adjusters, clergymen, young and old sportsmen with a piece of land, young women and mothers all acknowledge that this new Fiat is the long-awaited automobile at an affordable price, both in terms of operation and maintenance. It is not one of life's fleeting toys with limited possibilities, but a true, complete, superb automobile made to last and serve and to satisfy the most varied and demanding needs." With a total of 113,095 manufactured by 1937 in three- and four-speed versions, the Balilla was also successful abroad. It was built under license in Spain, Great Britain and Poland by Fiat Hispania, Fiat England and Fiat Polski, respectively; in Germany it was built by NSU while in France, this French Simca-made car was given the name 6CV.

100 This 1930s poster for Fiat also became an opportunity for Fascist propaganda. A young Balilla (the name given to members of the Italian Fascist Youth Movement aged 8-14) is in the foreground and the Balilla automobile is in the background. Benito Mussolini wanted to motorize Italy with this vehicle.

101 The Fiat Balilla Tre Marce, manufactured from 1932 to 1934, was the first series of a model created for mass motorization, thanks to its reasonable price (Lira 10,800), compact size, agility and operating affordability. It was the first Italian car with production in excess of 100,000 units.

There were two models in between the Balilla and the Topolino – Fiat's second milestone at the time. Following the success of the 508 Balilla, the Ardita was presented in 1933 and the 1500 in 1935 with the idea of expanding the range to include models in the mid and mid-to-high range. Despite the advertising hype claiming "It emerges and conquers," the Ardita didn't conquer a place in the sun. It had the opposite features of the Balilla (lackluster performance, elevated consumption and high maintenance costs), which resulted in only 8500 units being sold. However, the Ardita, and more particularly the 1500, started the stylistic evolution, making them modern vehicles and suddenly ageing all previous models. The six-seater 518L Ardita outfitted by Bertone was a limousine with rounded fenders (they still weren't integrated with the bodywork), a tilted windshield (no longer straight) and a front end whose radiator grill comprised the radiator. The bodywork of the 1500 (produced by Fiat to reme-

dy the Ardita flop) was winding and streamlined, the fenders were in even greater harmony with the hood and made room for the lights, which no longer protruded. The 1500 also offered a spacious driver and passenger compartment with room for five, a proportionate trunk, quarter vent windows, a hand brake that became a handle under the dashboard, automatic-return turn signals controlled by a specific lever on the steering wheel column and another lever that controlled flashing lights. These are all standard features on today's cars, but the 1500 offered them first, in addition to a six-cylinder, 1.5L (1.493 cc) engine, one of the smallest in the world and a mark of style – especially the front end – which would be used by and contribute to the success of the 500A Topolino. Another element that confirmed the vehicle's cutting edge was its period of production. The 1500 and its various series, A, B, C, D and E, remained in production for almost 15 years (1935-1948), accompanying Italians through

the war and the post-war periods. Like the 1500, the Topolino was also successful, as demonstrated by the 122,016 units sold between 1936 and 1948, in addition to the 20,000 units manufactured under license by NSU and Simca. Series B and C kept the Topolino in production until 1955, when it was replaced by the 600, by which time over half a million Topolino units had been manufactured, making it one of the undisputed protagonists of so-called mass motorization.

102-103 Sales of the Fiat 518 Ardita were not very successful. Production of the 1750, 2000 (corresponding to engine size) and the 527 Ardita 2500 versions, manufactured from 1934 to 1936, only totaled 8452 units.

103 This poster advertised the Fiat 518 Ardita, the mid-size vehicle produced in 1933 to control this market segment and take advantage of the Balilla's success.

The first secret of the 500 Topolino's success was the ability of its creator, engineer Dante Giocosa, another genius car designer who always tied his brilliance and talent to Fiat. Born in Rome in 1905 to a Piedmont family, he lived and worked in Turin and designed all Fiat models until 1971. He had the task of creating a very small automobile — the smallest in the world back then — on a chassis with a wheelbase only 6½ ft (2 m) long that was able to transport two adults and two children in addition to baggage. This became possible thanks to the technical solutions implemented (the engine's center of mass was outside the wheelbase and it had a single transversal leaf spring). However, its length (10½ ft or 3.21 m), a four-cylinder, 0.6L (569 cc), 13 hp engine, bonsai size and light weight (1179 lbs or 535 kg) allowed it to reach 53 mph (85 km/h). And that's not all — at a price of 8900 Lira, with average consumption exceeding 10 miles (16 km) per 0.22 gal (1 L), and with an annual road tax of just 275 Lira, it became the vehicle Agnelli wanted; a car for all families, even those with limited economic resources. As already mentioned, stylistically it drew from the 1500: rounded, the pre-series version even had lights integrated with the bodywork, but high production costs forced the classic solution to be used in the end. The Topolino was a nice-looking car, small and somewhat mouse-shaped (*topolino* is the Italian term for a little mouse) and was the result of a winning project.

The last new Fiat that left the factory before World War II broke out was the 2800. It was a company car created along the lines of the 1500C, offered in sedan and convertible versions and stood out for its majestic front end (drawn from again from the 1939 1100). The 2800 was the first model to leave the new factory in Mirafiori (which employed 22,000 workers at the time) and was practically a remake of the 508C to celebrate Fiat's 40th anniversary.

104 The head of the Fiat projects office, engineer Dante Giacosa, poses next to his invention, the Topolino. This vehicle represented his victory over the great challenge of creating the smallest four-seater (it was 10½ ft – 3.21 m – long).

105 Workers on Line 1 at Fiat's factory in Turin. The body of the 500A – better known as the Topolino – is about to be lowered onto the chassis.

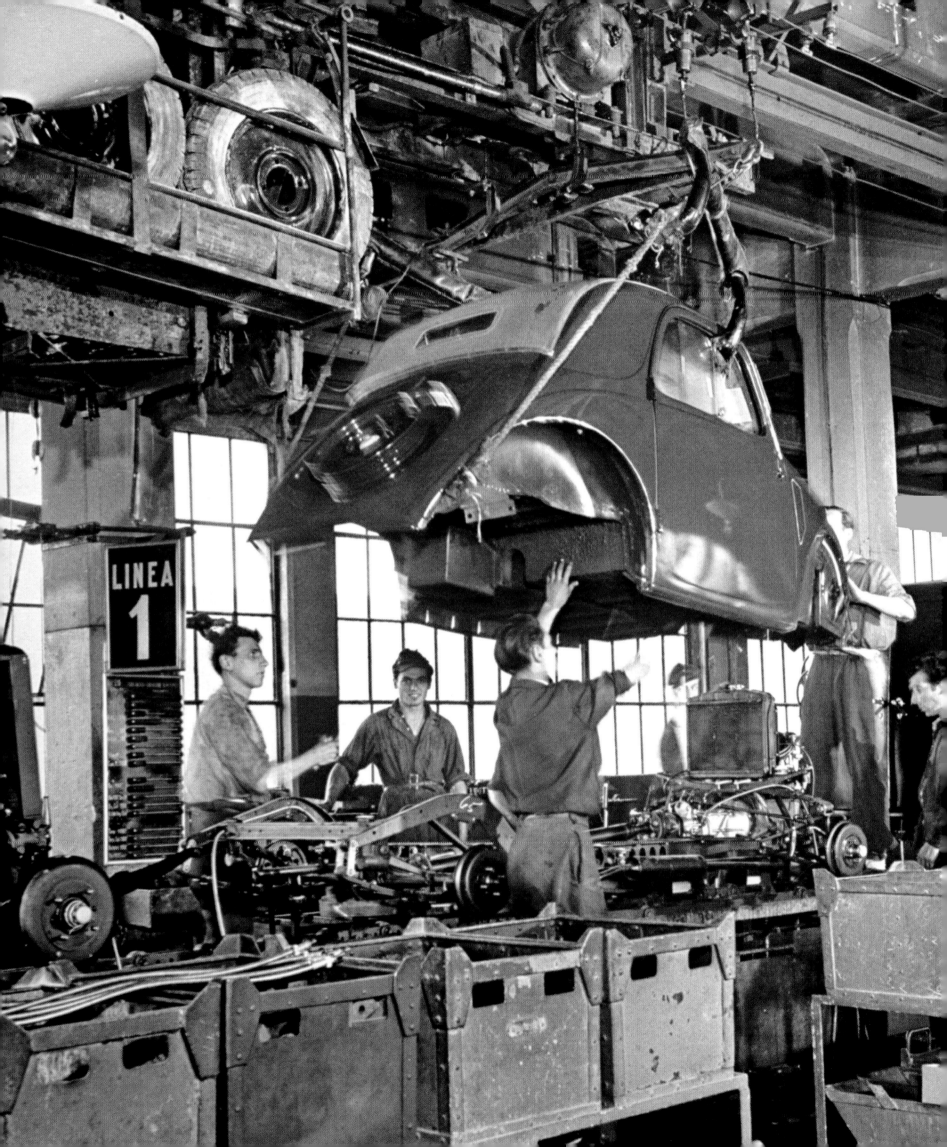

top version that almost made it a convertible. When it made its debut, it was the smallest four-seater in the world (fitting two adults and two children or baggage). It achieved this goal thanks to the position of the engine's center of mass outside the wheelbase and to the suspension front leaf springs, spring.

108-109 In 1941 Fiat produced a special model for King Umberto that was characterized by two large doors, which provided easy access (even to the back) and streamlined rear wheels with chrome inserts.

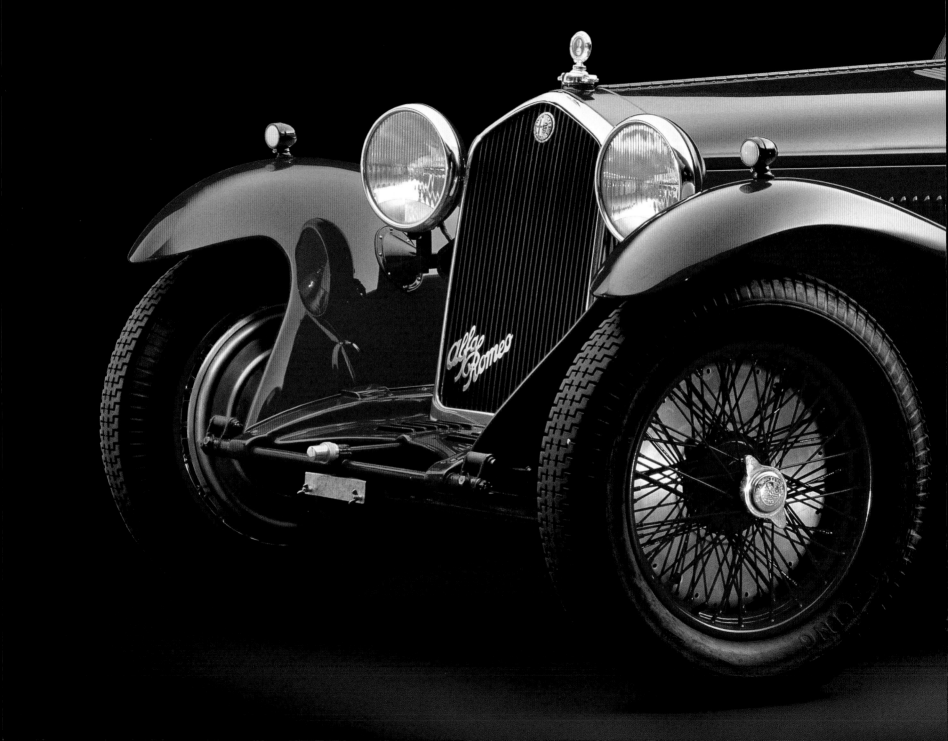

During this period, Alfa Romeo's mass production experienced the effects of its extraordinary successes in the competitive field. Races fell under Ferrari Team management, the *Prancing Stallion* took the place of the four-leaf clover and Enzo Ferrari distributed race models such as the Tipo B, Bimotore, Tipo 8C, Tipo 12C, and the 158 (better known as the Alfetta) prior to the war. The transfer to the Drake was one of the consequences of Alfa Romeo's industrial reorganization after the Milanese automaker was acquired by the Istituto di Riconversione Industriale.

In addition to renouncing the direct management of the races, reorganization also involved the sales network as branches fell under direct management by the parent company rather than private dealers. Special attention was also paid to producing commercial vehicles, buses, diesel engines and engines used in aviation, for which a specific plant was built in Pomigliano d'Arco (later destroyed by bombings).

The factories in Portello were also attacked, but its machinery had been safely stored beforehand and its 8000 workers returned to work at the end of the war. Only 10 percent of Alfa Romeo's work-ers actually manufactured automobiles. In this decade, models included another masterpiece by Jano, created in 1931, the 8C 2300-2600 and its successor, the 8C 2900 A-B in 1936, which took their place in the automobile world as high performing, grand touring vehicles. At the 1936's edition of the Mille Miglia, their barrel-shaped bodies conquered the entire podium as they greatly outdistanced the competition. To understand the value of the 8C in the history of Alfa Romeo, consider that in 2007 a brilliant performing GT returned under the same name.

110-111 The Alfa Romeo 8C 2300, seen here in the Spider version produced by Touring in 1934, participated in races right from the start. In 1931 two of Zagato's vehicles participated in the Mille Miglia registered by the Ferrari Team and driven by Nuvolari (grandfather) and Arcangeli (retired).

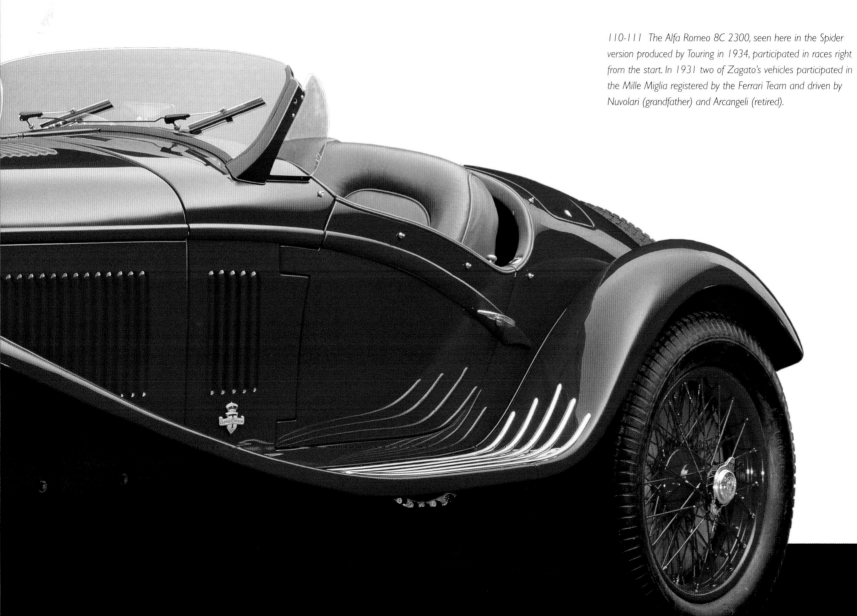

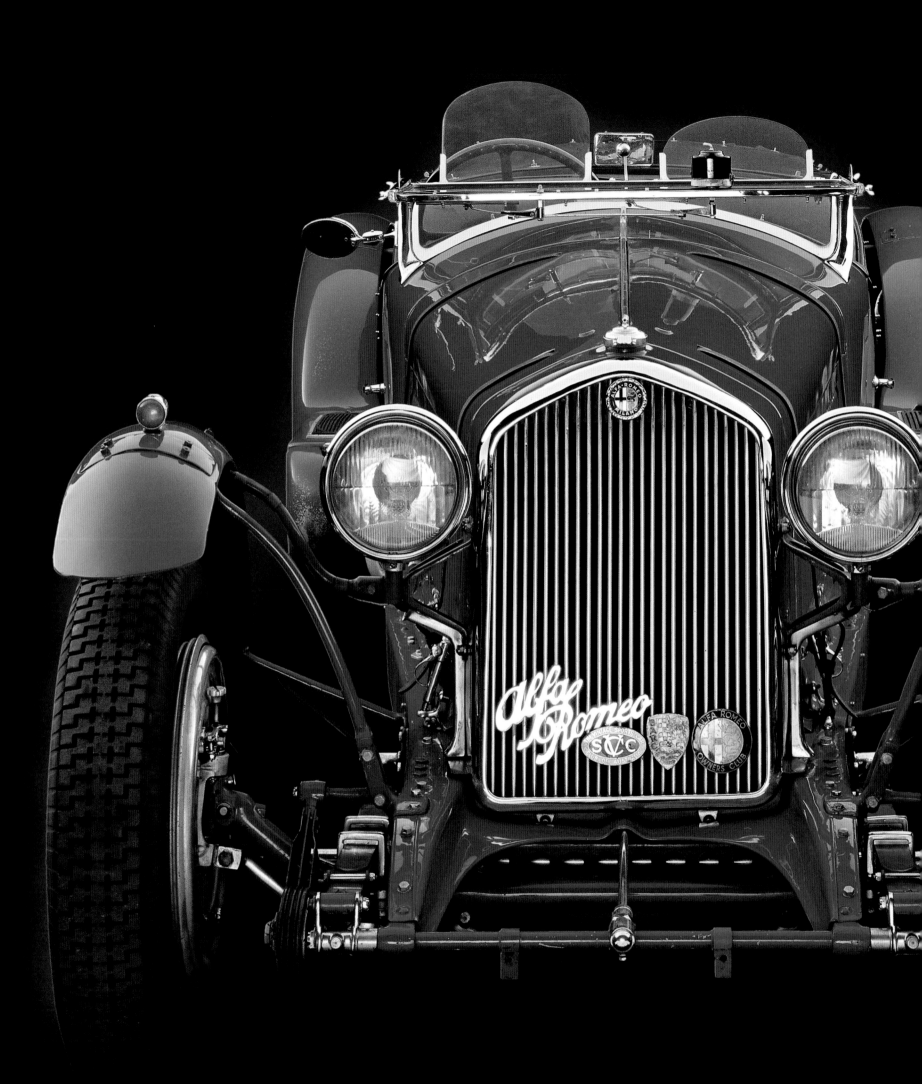

112-113 and 113 French sports vehicles are identified by the color blue, just as Italian cars are by red British cars by bottle-green. This is a 1933 Alfa Romeo 8C 2300 Le Mans by Touring, another vehicle intended to confirm Alfa Romeo's racing supremacy. One hundred and eighty-eight units were manufactured and equipped with a powerful eight-cylinder, 2.3L (2336 cc) 142 hp engine. The chassis used in race cars usually has a smaller wheelbase (distance between the wheel axles) than the one used for private, everyday road-legal vehicles. Unique features included a rear compartment for the spare tire.

114-115 and 115 top An
austere color, commanding size
and a fascinating shape, this
1938 Alfa Romeo 8C 2900B
was characterized by its very
long hood, which housed a 220
hp engine with two positive
displacement compressors (for
racing) and a very short back
end. These opposite proportions
gave this vehicle the charm for
which it has always been loved
and admired. Other interesting
streamlining features were the
fenders covering the rear
wheels and a curved trunk
that further highlighted its
decreased dimensions.

The 6C 1750 evolved into the 6C 1900 GT and 6C 2300 and 2300B manufactured between 1933 and 1939. In that year, 1939, further evolutions led to the 6C 2500, which proved to be a very capable and long-lived model whose improvements and updates allowed it to remain in production until 1953. Versions included the Coloniale version, with a top that could be opened and folded; it was intended specifically for the colonies and its internal mechanics had been partially modified to face the desert and bleak Ethiopian and Eritrean roads. Unfortunately, most of the 6C Coloniale vehicles ended up in Russia for the transportation of officers from the Armir expeditionary force. This caused some obvious difficulties, starting firstly with the very cold winter temperatures, which led to a four-wheel drive version with a short wheelbase, low pressure and grooved tires. The project did not make it to the mass-production lines, however, as the war was coming to a head.

116 The 1938 cover page of the magazine L'auto italiana shows a picture of a long Alfa Romeo 8C 2900B manufactured from 1937 to 1939.

116-117 This 1939 lightweight version of the Alfa Romeo 6C 2500 was called Superleggera and was one of this vehicle's many versions throughout its long career (as compared to Alfa standards). It remained in production until 1953 and led Alfa Romeo into the war.

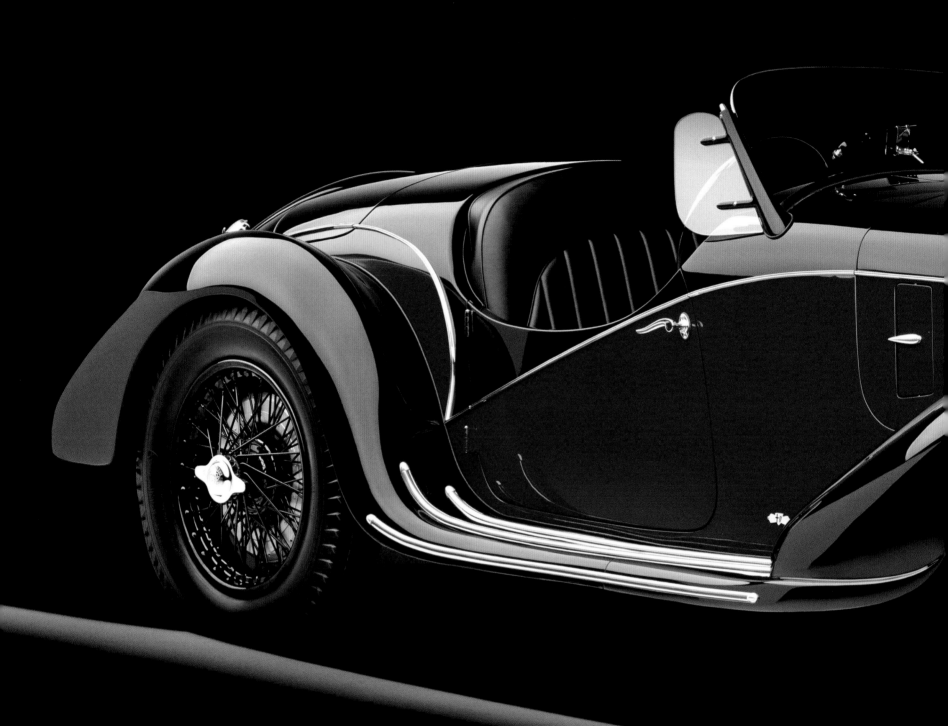

118-119 The Alfa Romeo 6C 2500 Super Sport made its debut in 1939 and was one of the versions entrusted to external car designers. Its wheelbase was nine feet long (2.7 m), unlike the Sport version, which was longer (10 ft or 3 m). The other, classic versions Turismo and Turismo six-seven-seater were designed in-house. They were all equipped with a six-cylinder 2.4L (2443 cc) engine whose performance was pleasing, and was an improvement over the 6C 2300B it replaced. This model also satisfied those looking for an elegant, exclusive and fast car. A total of 609 units were produced.

Ferrari, from Alfa Romeo to Auto Avio

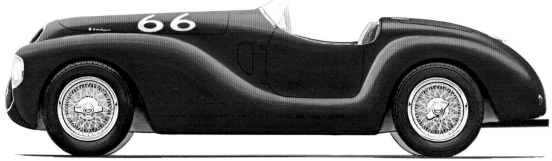

28.04.1940 - Mille Miglia - Auto Avio Costruzioni 815 - Ascari/Minozzi, rit.

Enzo Ferrari was appointed *commendatore* in 1927 but in 1938 disagreements with management caused him to abandon his job and Alfa Romeo. This action also forced him to promise to refrain from putting the Ferrari Team back together and from undertaking any racing activities for at least four years.

These reasons led him to establish Auto Avio Costruzioni, a company whose headquarters were in Modena in the same offices that were once home to the Ferrari Team, and whose corporate purpose was to build machine tools and components for aero engines. By doing this, the Drake circumvented the waiver he had signed with Alfa Romeo and devoted himself to realizing the 815 ordered by two wealthy young descendants of a family from Ferrara. They wanted it to race in the 1940 Brescia Grand Prix, which replaced the Mille Miglia (it had been interrupted two years earlier by serious accidents). Therefore, the 815 was Ferrari's first vehicle, even though his name couldn't appear anywhere on it. The name stood for an eight-cylinder, 1.5L (1500 cc) engine and was the first sign of an identification system that Ferrari enthusiasts would get to know. In order to build his 815, Ferrari collaborated with specialists such as Alberto Massimino, an engineer tech-

nician and his collaborator during Alfa races, and Felice Bianchi Anderloni, the founder of Carrozzeria Touring. The vehicle's engine was the result of the merger of two Fiat 1100 engines, the displacement of which was reduced from 2.2 to 1.5 liters (2200 cc to 1500 cc), and a chassis belonging to the 508C. Two units were built based on the requirements of the two clients. The one for Marquis Lotario Rangoni Macchiavelli was based on exclusive outfitting and valuable leather interior, whereas the version for Alberto Ascari, who was a great driver at heart, was sporty and therefore more basic.

The two 815 vehicles were tested on the Milano-Laghi highway and their surprising performance created high hopes for their use in the Brescia Grand Prix. Both were forced to withdraw from the race, but their dominance was total as the vehicles reached 109 mph (175 km/h). After these two 815 models, Ferrari returned to his company's machine tools. The war slowed down activities as the factory was bombarded, but Ferrari did not lose heart. He started working on a new race car bearing his name to be built after the war, in light of the fact that his agreement with Alfa Romeo had finally come to an end.

120-121 Enzo Ferrari test driving his team's Alfa Romeo eight-cylinder on July 25, 1924.

121 The Auto Avio Costruzioni 815 prepared by Enzo Ferrari for the 1940 Mille Miglia and driven by Ascari-Minozzi. They dominated the 1.5L (1500 cc) category but were forced to pull out of the race due to engine failure.

Vincenzo Lancia's last masterpieces

If Fiat continued to pursue widespread distribution with models sold in the hundreds of thousands, first with the Balilla and later with the Topolino, Lancia remained a sign of quality, elegance and exclusivity on four wheels, combined with cutting-edge technology and revolutionary innovations. These unavoidable features of each car leaving the Turinese brand's factories were the reason why it remained unaffected by the difficult economic and financial times. Despite this, Vincenzo Lancia was aware of the scars left by the economic crisis on the wallets of the Italian people and asked his design engineers to create an affordable model without compromising the brand's quality. The market needed compact models, both in terms of dimension and engine size, which could provide adequate performance combined with contained consumption and lower maintenance costs, all without sacrificing space in the driver and passenger compartments or in the trunk. The answer from the Lancia technicians was originally called the Progetto 231 and later became the *vettura leggera Lancia* (light Lancia vehicle). Following

tradition, it was presented at the Paris Auto Show in 1932 to get a feel for the audience's reaction and those involved in the project. The following year the project was renamed Augusta in its permanent version at the Milan Auto Show. This was another milestone for the brand and the automobile itself, as it was the first sedan in the world with a monocoque body. The body, engine compartment, roof and trunk were all one; it was so solid that the central upright was eliminated, allowing the mounting of pillarless doors. Other innovations from a mechanical perspective included hydraulic brakes, which Vincenzo tested personally, making Lancia the first company in Europe to mount them. The Augusta met the affordability requirement without giving up style and excellent manufacturing, as expected by Lancia's demanding clientele. Certainly the Augusta was an example of the modern, compact economy car (12 feet or 3.81 m long) at an affordable price (19,500 Lira) and provided interesting performance and consumption (65 mph 105 km/h and 5½ miles or 9 km with 0.22 gal or 1 L) thanks to its 1.1L (1100 cc) engine. Before the Augusta, Lancia also presented the Artena and Astura, in 1931. These were mid-category models at affordable prices (31-45,000 Lira) whose names no longer referred to the Greek alphabet but respectively to the ancient city of the Voscians and a famous castle close to Nettuno. They were the first models to have pillarless doors, thanks to their rigid body. The Astura was like a big sister to the Artena, and despite the difficult economic times and a road tax based not only on engine size but also on the number of cylinders, it was offered with an eight-cylinder engine and a chassis, to the delight of all coachbuilders, who were up to their necks in requests to personalize this elegant and reliable vehicle. Touring, Farina and Pinin Farina and Castagna created sedans and convertibles and even a very long six-seater coupe. For its part, the Artena stood out for its reliability, so much so that its four-cylinder, narrow V engine was guaranteed to run 62,135 miles (100,000 km) without the need for servicing. And then there was the Aprilia, which, at the will of its founder, had to be a light, aerodynamic five-door sedan, provide excellent performance, be stable, easy to handle and suitable for those looking for affordable sportiness and elegance, not weigh more than 1984 lbs (900 kg) and be equipped with a contained engine size. Once again, the results were extraordinary. The vehicle was presented in 1937 with modern, round shapes, a sloping tail end and rounded top in addition to pillarless doors, independent suspension and an engine size slightly bigger than that of the Augusta (1.2L or 1200 cc). It was a success. Sales took off and continued until 1949 when it was replaced by the Aurelia. Coachbuilders once again had a great time personalizing them, sporting successes were countless and the second series in 1939 boasted a bigger engine. However, Vincenzo Lancia could not enjoy any of this. He died in 1937 at the age of only 56, before the Aprilia was ever marketed.

122-123 The Lancia Augusta made its debut in 1932, as usual at the Paris Auto Show, although it was named the vettura leggera Lancia (light Lancia vehicle) at the time. Its official name only appeared the next year at the Milan Auto Show.

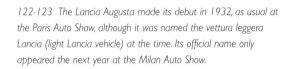

124-125 and 125 top
The Lancia Ardea made its
debut in 1939 and remained
in production until 1953.
Production was forced to stop
due to the war, but this fact
did not halt its development. It
was presented again at the
end of the war with an
improved transmission, which
became five-gear and led to
contained consumption that
made it highly sought-after by
taxi drivers, and also offered
a van body outfitting. This
vehicle was created as a
small luxury car to replace
the Augusta.

126-127 The Lancia Astura was manufactured from 1931 to 1937 and received its name from a well known castle close to Nettuno (Rome). It was equipped with an eight-cylinder engine and evolved from the Artena but with a longer chassis.

Great drivers and
memorable sporting achievements

Alfa Romeo, Enzo Ferrari, the Ferrari Team, the Mille Miglia, Tazio Nuvolari, Achille Varzi and Giuseppe Farina. These names need no introduction and helped to write the history of international motor racing. This was an extraordinary period for races and their protagonists. Just think of Nuvolari (also known as Nivola or the Flying Mantuan) at the wheel. Many feel that he was, is and will always be the greatest driver ever. He was fearless, drove very fast, first motorcycles and then cars, and he did it despite his age. He was 28 when he started racing motorcycles and 38 when he took the wheel of the Alfa 6 C 1750 for the Mille Miglia, but he had speed in his blood, was impulsive (today we would say he takes each corner sideways) and was exuberant and charismatic. Listing his achievements would require a separate volume, but one example of Nuvolari's brilliance was at Nürburgring in 1935. That day Tazio decided to win in Germany and against Mercedes' Germans, and he openly said so before the beginning of the race. They were very lucky and their vehicle was superior to Nuvolari's Alfa, but his words were not

empty and he won. The Germans had to withdraw during the last lap, lower the German flag from the flagpole and find the Italian national anthem to replace the German one, which was all ready to be played over the loudspeakers. After a moment of despair, the crowd hailed him and bore him shoulder-high. Nuvolari was a hero whose gestures were endless. He would have been happy to die on the track, like his arch-rival, the cold and calculating

Achille Varzi. Instead, Nuvolari died in his bed in 1953 after a long illness and three years after his last race. The golden years of racing in the thirties were stopped by the war, but the passion for racing was not lost and when the war was over, great racing drivers and vehicles were ready and waiting. The Formula One World Championship made its debut in 1950 and was won by Alfa Romeo that year and the following year.

130 A smiling, satisfied Tazio Nuvolari held shoulder-high after crossing the finish line in first place (on a Bugatti Gran Sport) at the third Circuito Automobilistico di Roma – Premio Reale.

131 Tazio Nuvolari the tightrope walker on two wheels. This great, unforgettable Italian race-car driver was born in Castel d'Ario in the province of Mantua in 1892 and died after a long illness in Mantua in 1953.

132 top Achille Varzi on a single-seater Alfa Romeo P3, which, like its precursor P2, continued winning races and asserting itself with the same authority and power by winning virtually all the races it entered between 1932 to 1934.

132 bottom Achille Varzi sitting in a group photograph between the wheel of the Bugatti Gran Sport and his trusted mechanic Gianella at the end of a race. Varzi was one of the great Italian race-car drivers in the 1930s.

133 A tired Achille Varzi with Arcangeli, who can be recognized by his Maserati overalls. Arcangeli was immortalized after he completed the Monza Grand Prix in the early 1930s.

CHAPTER 4

Reconstruction began with the old models

Italy didn't exactly start over from scratch after World War II, but it wasn't far off. The country was disfigured by bombings and automakers' factories were one of the sensitive targets because they had produced war material, from trucks to airplane engines and ammunition. As in other countries, ideas and projects were set in motion during the recovery, starting with pre-war models that were duly updated. Car designers proposed new models with more streamlined and reactive structures, perhaps by exploiting a chassis that was buried in the back of the warehouse somewhere. However, the trend was marked and continued in the wake of the transformations that had been un-

derway during the 1930s. Automobiles took the shapes we are used to seeing today, with bodies integrating all those elements that were originally separate from the vehicle's bodywork, such as the radiator, lights and fenders, giving life in the fifties to what designers refer to as the fourth phase, that is, the modern car.

Italy was among the leaders despite starting with a handicap; in fact, it was precisely this disadvantage that spurred on the automobile industry. Its car designers and stylists created vehicles that symbolized the history of the car and led the country through the 1950s, the first decade in which more than 100,000 vehicles were sold in Italy (112,110 in 1953), which towards the end of the decade, led to mass motorization and the economic boom that continued through 1964. In 1958 the Italian market delivered 830,175 vehicles and over a million in 1966. Up to that point, Italy – which had a developed system of automobile distribution – was still behind other European countries in terms of motorization. Despite this, increased motorization not only meant organizing a suitable roadway network that was able to move traffic, but also meeting the need to travel quickly in a car, thanks to the performance of the models of the time.

The endeavors of Italian vehicles and racing drivers in international races spurred motorists further. The *Autostrada del Sole* highway was built, the result of an impressive policy to build highways, unrivalled in Europe and later known as the *Fanfani Plan*. The first stone was laid on May 19, 1956 and started a plan that provided for roadways in excess of 3311 miles (5329 km). The development of Italy on four wheels had begun, never to be stopped. Until the 1970s, with its oil shocks and Sundays on foot, no war or crisis for 30 years could stop this development, which allowed Italy to express itself in terms of the automobile.

However, this period is also remembered for all the deaths that the Italian world of engines brought with it. When Giovanni Agnelli died in 1945, his dear, faithful friend Vittorio Valletta was named president of Fiat in his place. Valletta had

started with the company in 1921 as an administrative manager and was able to carry Fiat through years of crisis, providing it with the growth it needed to survive, indulge mass motorization and make a permanent mark on the international automobile scene.

In 1947, it was the turn of Ettore Bugatti. The death of this genius and his farewell to his

beloved birthplace of Milan (although he was buried in the family tomb in Dorlisheim, close to Molsheim) led to the permanent decline of his car manufacturing company. It had already sustained a serious blow with the death of his son Jean in 1937 while test driving the Tipo 57 close to the factory in Molsheim. Many racing drivers lost their lives, while racing or just taking a test drive. Racing without limits and without the safety and protection we take for granted today, was very risky. Often it took the death of these drivers to establish a vehicle's maximum speed. In a way, perhaps it was better like this. The ego and passion reached a climax when they left the scene, like heroes on the field of battle, rather than like common mortals in a bed.

134-135 The 1958 Ferrari 250 GT Coupe Tour de France race version. Unlike road-legal versions, this one was equipped with a small wheelbase for increased agility.

136 A Fiat 500 with a full load on the roof. This small Fiat started its brilliant career in 1957; it had room for four, but finding room for luggage was certainly a challenge.

136-137 A Fiat Topolino and 1100B in the Piazza Duomo in Milan in front of the cathedral. These are the 1950s and traffic wasn't as chaotic as it is today.

Cisitalia 202 and Ferrari 166: the first modern sports cars were born

Historians and designers agree that the Cisitalia 202 was the archetype of the modern sports vehicle, along with the Ferrari 166 MM and Maserati A6 1500. All three cars were Italian, and all three captivated the automotive world. This is not simply patriotic pride, because these three vehicles changed the design of the automobile and became the starting point for new developments. The Cisitalia (an abbreviated form of Compagnia Industriale Sportiva Italiana) 202 was established in 1946 at the behest of Turinese industrialist and enthusiast Piero Dusio and racing driver Piero Taruffi, who wanted to create Grand Prix sports cars that were accessible to anyone who wanted to participate in the races. Their dream became reality with the D46 designed first by Dante Giacosa and then by Giovanni Savonuzzi when Giacosa returned to Fiat. The D46's motor was derived from the Fiat 1100. and allowed the vehicle to reach 106 mph (170 km/h), but the importance of this model was that it became the basis for the 202 created in 1947, which was streamlined, harmonious, low, curvaceous and had large glass surface areas. In short, this sports car was so beautiful that it was elevated to a work of art, in 1951 it was displayed in the permanent collections of New York's MOMA as a moving sculpture. It was also the undisputed star during its unofficial debut in 1947 at the Italian Grand Prix and the Villa d'Este Concours d'Elégance. The shapes of the 202 were designed by Pinin Farina, while Savonuzzi suggested creating a car as large as a Buick, as low as a GP model, as comfortable as a Rolls-Royce and as light as the D46. Despite a price tag of 6800 dollars, many examples were sold overseas, and even Henry Ford II bought two of them. Cisitalia reached an agreement with Mr. Ford in 1951 to produce the 808XF, with a chassis by Savonuzzi, bodywork by Ghia, and equipped with an eight-cylinder Ford Mercury engine. However, the contract was short lived and only 188 units were produced. On the other hand, a total of 221 units of the 202 model

were built between 1947 and 1953, including Pinin Farina and Vignale's coupe and Pinin Farina, Stabilimenti Farina and Castagna's convertible. The 202 SMM version (the Mille Miglia open two-seater, also referred to as the Nuvolari Spider because the Flying Mantuan took it to second place in the 1947 Mille Miglia) were also by Stabilimenti Farina. This latter vehicle and its 65 hp engine (which belonged to the Fiat 1100) reached 112 mph (180 km/h) against the coupe's 99 mph (160 km/h). In 1953 the Dusio family left Cisitalia, marking the beginning of the company's decline, which culminated with it closing down in 1964 after a series of unsuccessful models.

138 The 1947 Cisitalia 202 left its mark on post-war automobile design. It was created by Pinin Farina and in 1951 was permanently displayed at New York's MOMA with the title Sculpture in Movement.

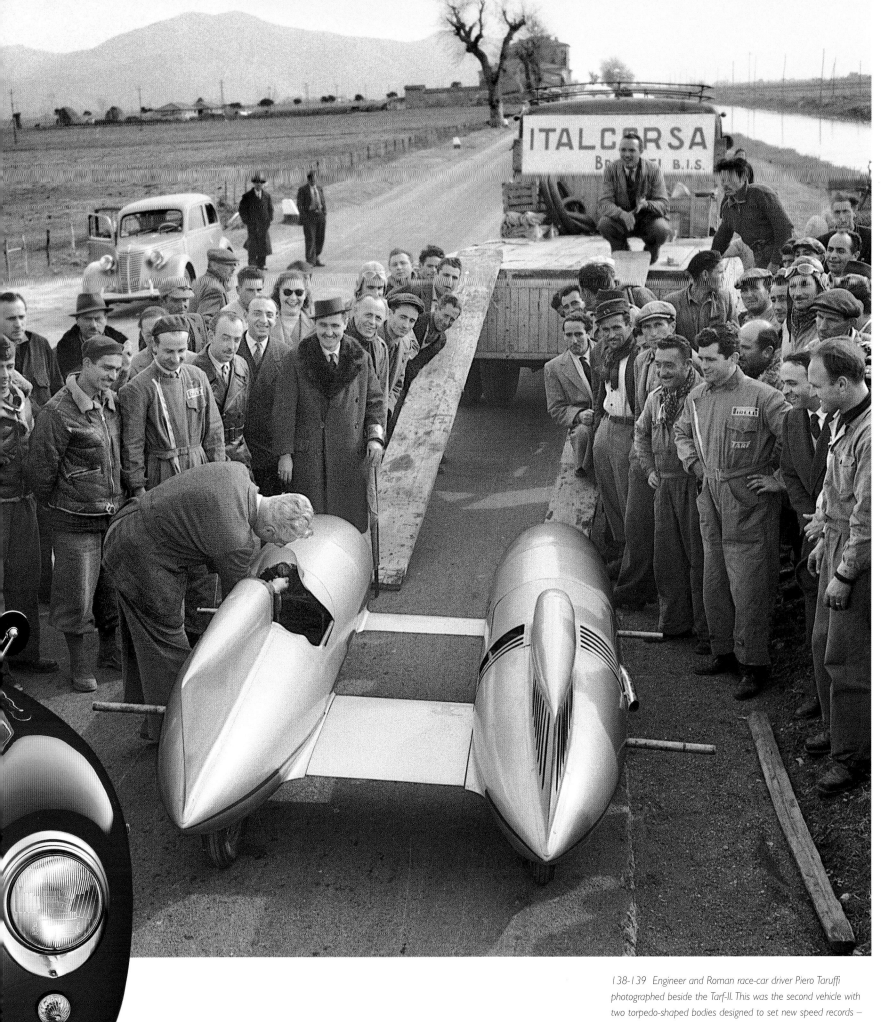

138-139 Engineer and Roman race-car driver Piero Taruffi photographed beside the Tarf-II. This was the second vehicle with two torpedo-shaped bodies designed to set new speed records – the same records he tried to set on a motorcycle.

140-141 and 141 top
The Cisitalia 202 SMM, or Spider
Mille Miglia, was manufactured
in 1947 by manufacturer Farina,
but it was better known as the
Spider Nuvolari in honor of the
Mantuan race-car driver who
immediately conquered second
place at the Mille Miglia that
same year. The front and tail
ends of the marvelous vehicle
depicted in these photographs
is equipped with chassis no.
001 and engine no. 006.

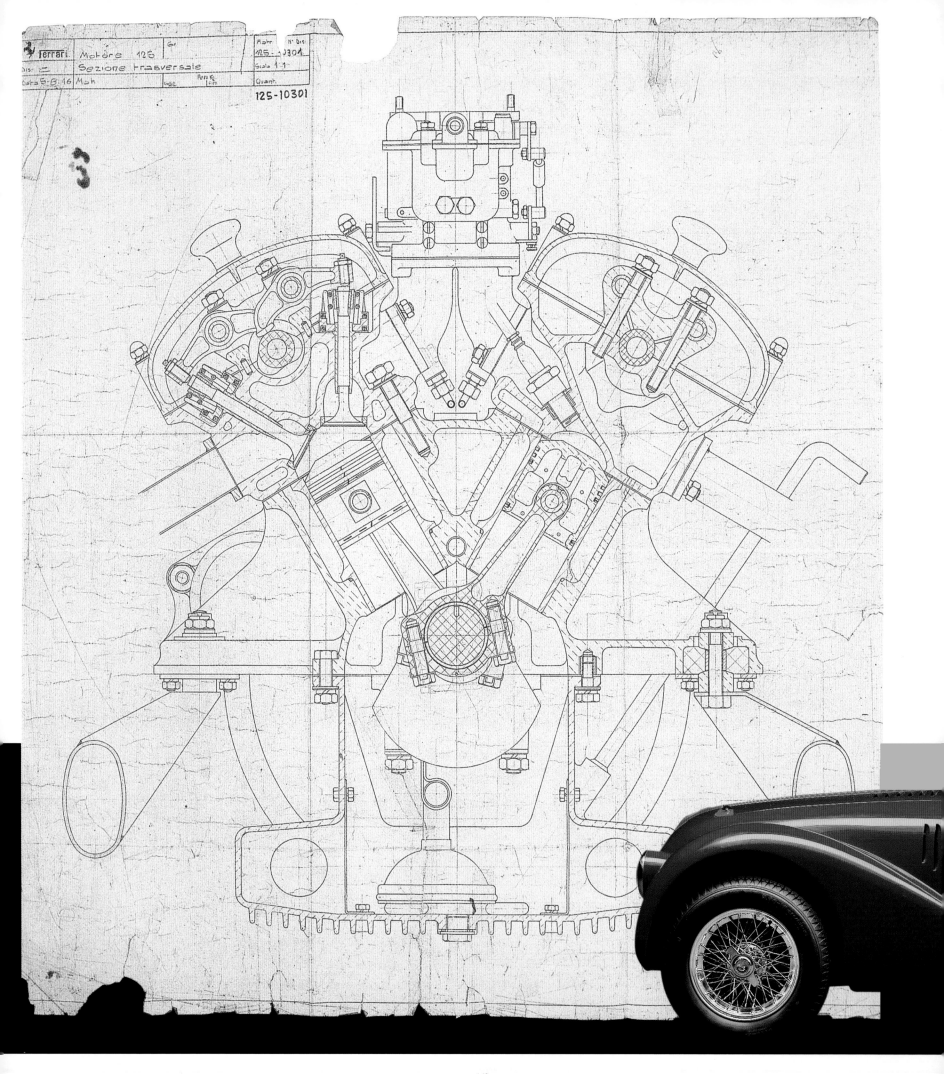

Ferrari, on the other hand, became the most famous automaker in the world with its second model, the 166. This vehicle provided the world with another example of a sports car in terms of shapes and performance that is still current today. After the Auto Avio play described in the previous chapter, the restrictions on Enzo Ferrari resulting from his stormy departure from Alfa Romeo, the company that had launched his career as a test driver and with which he had collaborated for two decades, had ended, albeit after a hefty severance penalty. This meant that Enzo could finally put his name on his own cars, and Ferrari officially opened in Maranello in 1946. The Drake transferred the workshop from Modena to Maranello during the war. Its first vehicle, the 125 S, marked its debut with a new 12-cylinder engine in 1947 on the Piacenza circuit with a victory. This was the first of a series of victories that would permanently bring the brand to the top of the world. The name Ferrari and the black prancing stallion finally appeared, an emblem that represented the airplanes used during World War I by pilot Francesco Baracca and given to Ferrari by Baracca's family in memory of their son. The yellow background behind the stallion was Ferrari's idea because the color represented the city of Modena. The 125 was the first of a series of models that intertwined their history with races (described in detail elsewhere). Road-legal production versions of the 166 were manufactured in 1948. The Inter coupe, designed by Touring Superleggera, was the first Ferrari not intended to race. In fact, it had a

comfortable compartment for a driver and a passenger, a very narrow space in the back for two more passengers and a modern, streamlined profile similar to that of a sporty modern car. It had a long front end, ovoid radiator grill and rounded tail end. In addition to the Inter were the S, F2 and Mille Miglia versions and the Touring against which Vignale, Bertone and Stabilimenti Farina pitted themselves. Later versions derived from the 166 included the

195 Inter, 212 Inter and 340-342 America. The latter name indicated that the model was designed for the United States, a market Ferrari viewed with extreme interest. To this end, Luigi Chinetti (a personal friend of the Drake) moved overseas and founded the North American Racing Team so that young, talented individuals could race with Maranello's red cars, but also to sell Ferrari production models in their specific America versions.

144 and 145 bottom This is one of the many versions of the Ferrari 166, which was manufactured from 1947 to 1951. Specifically, this is a Spider Corsa equipped with a 12-cylinder V engine. The reason for the numerous versions is that Ferrari chassis are fitted to order and often have a unique shape and outfitting.

145 top Enzo Ferrari speaking confidentially with Mercedes team manager Alfred Neubauer in 1953 at the Italian Monza Grand Prix during a test session. The conversation concerned the Drake, who was thinking about retiring from the race after a series of accidents had led to the death of some of his racing drivers. Unfortunately, this was quite normal for the times.

This brings us to the first refined, fast and elegant GT models that were comfortable on the road: the 250 Europa with a V12, 3.0L (3000 cc) engine, designed by Gioacchino Colombo, and the 375 America with a V12, 4.5L (4500 cc) engine, designed by Aurelio Lampredi. These vehicles marked the beginning of collaboration with Pinin Farina, bodywork that, when combined with Colombo's engine, gave life to a broad and well known series of both road-legal and track models. These started with the 250 (1954) in various versions: the Europa, Boano-Ellena, GT PF E GTE 2+2, up to the GT Berlinetta with its short wheelbase, the GT Lusso in production until 1963-1964, and the Testa Rossa, 410 Superamerica, plus the legendary and highly sought after California LWB (long wheelbase) and SWB (short wheelbase). In May of 2008, on the occasion of the *Leggenda e passione* auction organized in Maranello by RM Auction in collaboration with Sotheby's, BBC star Chris Evans bought a no. 13 (of a total of 56 produced between 1960 and 1963) black 250 California SWB once owned by actor James Coburn, who purchased it second-hand in 1964 after filming *The Great Escape*. The sale price was 7.04 million euros, the highest amount ever paid for a mass-produced Ferrari (in fact, the auction house quoted between 4-6 million euros). This recent sale explains this vehicle's timeless fascination. Just imagine that when it made its debut, Hollywood actors and even Victor Emanuel of Savoy and Brigitte Bardot bought one, and the French actress later bought a second one. The first 250 GT convertible in 1957 was ordered by the Aga Khan.

146-147 The Spider 250 California, a Ferrari icon and sought-after model by collectors world-wide (the 1958 model shown here is equipped with a long wheelbase). Forty-nine units were produced and permanently opened the door to the United States for the prancing stallion.

148-149 It's true that the Ferrari is traditionally red, but this yellow 250 GT Swb, with a short wheelbase, just 8 feet (2.4 m) long, simply confirms the charm of this vehicle, which at the end of the 1950s was the fastest in the world, reaching a maximum speed of 119 mph (210 km/h).

150-151 The 1959 Ferrari 410 Superamerica was intended for the American market. This was the last of four years of production during which time 36 closed and convertible units were manufactured with wheelbases 8½ and nine feet long (2.6 and 2.8 m). Designed and produced by Pinin Farina, this coupe could reach 162 mph (260 km/h) and was equipped with a V12 5.0L (4962 cc) engine.

A Maserati for the Shah

The Shah of Persia ordered one of the most prestigious Maserati models at the time. The very elegant and fast 1959 5000 GT sports car (clients could personalize it by directly dealing with the coachbuilder) was equipped with an eight-cylinder engine taken from the race versions and its bodywork was first created by Touring and later by Pinin Farina, Ghia, Frua, Monterosa and Allemano. Of the total 34 units produced, one came off the production lines with no words or *Tridente* logos; this one was for Fiat deputy chairman Gianni Agnelli. Postwar, Maserati was managed by the Orsi family after it had taken the company over from the Maserati brothers in 1937, although the brothers continued collaborating until 1947 as managers of the engineering department. That was also the year that the A6 1500 made its debut, giving the sporty 6CM a commercial outlet. This was another shining example of a streamlined sporty vehicle with a long front end and recessed lights, which gave way to a series of elegant GT models allowing the automaker to carve out a niche for itself in this market segment. After the 1951 A6G 2000 and 1954 54, the 3500 GT made its debut in 1957 and encountered significant success (1972 units were manufactured), pulling the company out of the economic crisis in which it had found itself. This vehicle confirmed that Maserati was synonymous with elegant, streamlined, comfortable and fast vehicles that were easy to drive.

152-153 The bodywork of this 1954 Maserati A6 GCS is by Pinin Farina. The car made its debut together with the A6 1500 and immediately won the Modena Circuit (with Ascari behind the wheel). It was equipped with a six-cylinder cast-iron engine (cast iron in Italian is ghisa, hence the G in the name).

Fiat's fabulous 50s

After an uncertain post-war period and the death of Giovanni Agnelli in 1945, the succession of Vittorio Valletta to the leadership of Fiat allowed the company to overcome the difficult post-war years and experience unprecedented growth in the 1950s. It was a decade full of records. In 1953 the 1400 diesel was the first Italian diesel-operated car. The 1955 600 could easily seat four and, at an irresistible price of 590,000 Lira, it became the symbol of the Italian boom and sold 2.6 million units. The 1956 600 Multipla was the world's first minivan, and was closer to today's concept of a minivan than Ricotti's Siluro. The 1957 500 (once again a product of the genius Giocosa) does not really need any introduction, but it is worth mentioning that it was heir to the Topolino and won the Compasso d'Oro Design Award in 1959. It remained in production for 15 years until 1972 (over three million units were manufactured) and made a comeback fifty years later with the same original profiles. The odds are it will repeat its original success. From a corporate perspective, the success of Fiat's models translated into a decade with a workforce that grew from 60,000 to 80,000 employees, annual production that increased from 70,800 units in 1949 to 339,300 in 1958 and new factories being opened in southern Italy and overseas (Argentina, Yugoslavia, Mexico, South Africa and Turkey).

154 top Vittorio Valletta was appointed chairman of Fiat in 1946 following the death of Giovanni Agnelli. Behind him is a picture of the Mirafiori plants, which were doubled in 1958 and employed over 50,000 workers.

154 bottom Gianni Agnelli, with the President of the Italian Republic, Luigi Einaudi,

cuts the ribbon to inaugurate the 37th International Auto Show in Turin in front of a cross-section of a Fiat 600.

155 Italian actors Ugo Tognazzi (in the car) and Raimondo Vianello joke in a Fiat 600. It is 1957, two years after the car made its debut, which replaced the Topolino and replicated its great success.

156, 156-157 and 157 The heir and evolved version of the Siluro Ricotti based on a 1914 Alfa 40-60 HP, the Fiat 600 Multipla was the family version of the small 600 and made its debut in 1956 with an original line and practicality that rightfully made it the pioneer of the modern minivan. It seated up to six people in two rows and also had room for luggage. It was Giacosa's creation and was equipped with the same engine as the 600 (0.6L or 600 cc) and 24 hp, which, starting with the D version in 1960 was increased to 0.7L (767 cc) and 29 hp. The fuel tank was also increased from 7.1 to 7.6 gallons (27 to 29 liters). It was manufactured until 1966, including taxi and van body outfit versions.

158-159 *Fiat 500 parade along the streets of Turin in 1957, the year this new, small vehicle that would become the Turinese manufacturer's icon made its debut. However, the beginning of its brilliant career was somewhat difficult because it only cost a little less than the 600 (490,000 Lira compared to 640,000 Lira), it was very basic and its side windows were fixed (only the deflectors could be opened).*

160 top and 161 These posters illustrated the quality of the Fiat 500. The cloth roof over the front seats started appearing in 1959. The 500 D made its debut in 1960 and caused sales to take off. The vehicle was more comfortable, more accessorized, had a back seat that truly seated two and was equipped with a 0.5L (499.5 cc) engine taken from the 500 Sport with 17.5 hp, which allowed it to reach 59 mph (95 km/h) with reduced consumption: 12 miles with 0.26 gallons (20 km per liter).

160 bottom This was the last version of the small Fiat, the 500F, which was manufactured from 1965 to 1972. 2,272,092 units were manufactured in addition to the 821,557 units of the Nuova 500 and 500D versions. This vehicle immediately asserted itself as the most sold car in Italy.

Strictly from a production perspective, this Turinese company cannot only be considered as an economy-car manufacturer. The 1100, the first model produced from scratch after the war, was a mid-size car. Its new version was permanently approved in 1953, while six years later it was the turn of models in the mid-to-high range, such as the 1800 and 2100, the latter becoming the official car of many top Italian politicians. There was also the 1900, a reliable yet original sedan available in a very American-like Granluce coupe version, or the Torpedo Polizia, only for use by the Italian traffic police. One should not forget the Campagnola, the 1951 off-road vehicle that was Italy's response to the American Willys Jeep, which had a military version Ar (reconnaissance motor vehicle) and rivaled the 500. It made a great comeback in 2008, launched by Iveco as a variation of the Massif off-road vehicle and following the same philosophy of being hard, pure and basic. There was also room for the 1952 streamlined, aerodynamic 8V sports car, a descendant of Pinin Farina's 1100ES, which was named after the division of the same name. The 1100ES had an engine cylinder layout that guaranteed first-class performance for a vehicle superbly interpreted by car designers such as Zagato, Ghia and Vignale and could compete with Alfa Romeo and Ferrari.

162 top Actress Gina Lollobrigida gets into the Nuova Fiat 1100 four-door, mid-size sedan that replaced the 1100E. It was manufactured until 1963, including the last D version, which was available in sedan or station wagon versions (the latter being the most sold version of the entire range of models).

162 bottom Venetian background to the 1960 Fiat 500 Giardiniera, the 500 station wagon manufactured under the trademark Fiat until 1967 and then Autobianchi until 1977.

163 1950 Fiat 1400 poster making reference to the origins of the brand and the fist 3½ HP from 1899. This vehicle's rounded shapes were slightly reminiscent of the fashion at the time in the US. A diesel version was also manufactured in 1953 and 1954.

Italy's fiancée, the Giulietta and the avant-gardist Aurelia

164 top View of the 40th International Auto Show in Turin in 1958. In the foreground, the Alfa Romeo stand with different versions of the Giulietta. In the background, Fiat and the 600D Multipla.

Alfa Romeo and Lancia shared a common destiny after the war, that of having to deal with the destruction of their plants after the bombings and to begin reconstruction so they could be ready for market recovery. For the Milanese automaker, this meant getting more than 40 percent of their plants back on their feet, so production started up again with the 6C 2500 and only a thousand or so employees. The 1950s changed everything, however, from the models to the way they were produced. This was thanks to Orazio Satta Puliga who favored the introduction of the manufacturer's first mass assembly line to build the 1900, the first Alfa with a monocoque body.

The success of this new model was fundamental for the company's survival and it was also just as necessary to produce models in large quantities at a competitive price while remaining faithful to the brand's DNA. The 1951 1900 completely hit home as its slogan, "*The family car that wins races,*" hit the mark. It was in fact a comfortable mid-size sedan that seated five to six people, was easy to handle and was equipped with a powerful four-cylinder, twin-shaft engine (the only one in the world). Its 1.9L (1884 cc) engine and 90 hp provided excellent performance (93 mph or 150 km/h) combined with exemplary road holding, and was therefore level with the "racing" fame the brand had gained from competitions. The engine was also mounted on the Matta, that is the 1900M or AR51, an off-road vehicle used for military purposes which, like the Fiat Campagnola, was intended as a response to the excessive power of Willys. The 1900C 52 Disco Volante made history with its squat, shapely aluminum bodywork, by Touring Superleggera. It was intended for sport races and in fact was never produced nor used in races, but its results from a stylistic perspective are worth a standing ovation. There were also the futuristic BAT models (Berlinetta Aerodinamica Tecnica), developed by Bertone and based on the 1900.

Between the sedan, TI (Turismo Internazionale) Super, Sprint and Super Sprint and the 1900 otherwise known as the *Alfona*, it experienced eight honorable years (it also served as the Italian police car also known as the *Pantera*). A total of 19,039 units were manufactured despite the fact it was not permanently produced on the assembly line because some phases were still performed manually due to a lack of specialized machines.

164-165 The 1954 Alfa Romeo 1900 SSZ Super Sprint Zagato with a Touring version, the coupe of a sedan model dating back to 1951 that became well known for being used by the Italian Police, and was given the nickname Pantera (Panther).

166-167 and 167 A prototype and a scale model both developed based on the Alfa Romeo Giulietta model, which were the respective precursors of Pinin Farina's 1955 Spider (which was successful world-wide, especially in the United States) and Bertone's Sprint. The Spring was so successful at its presentation at the 1954 Turin Auto Show that 700 units were ordered immediately.

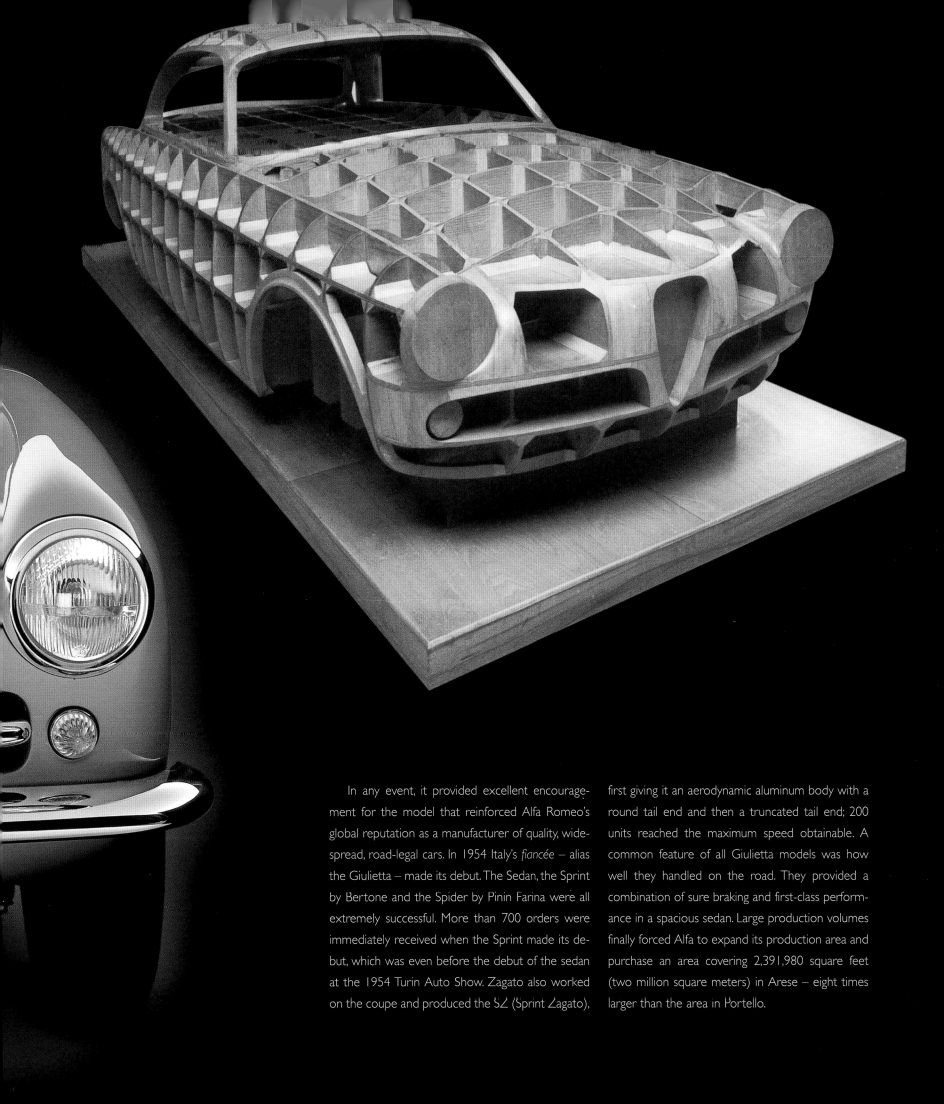

In any event, it provided excellent encourage-ment for the model that reinforced Alfa Romeo's global reputation as a manufacturer of quality, wide-spread, road-legal cars. In 1954 Italy's *fiancée* – alias the Giulietta – made its debut. The Sedan, the Sprint by Bertone and the Spider by Pinin Farina were all extremely successful. More than 700 orders were immediately received when the Sprint made its de-but, which was even before the debut of the sedan at the 1954 Turin Auto Show. Zagato also worked on the coupe and produced the SZ (Sprint Zagato),

first giving it an aerodynamic aluminum body with a round tail end and then a truncated tail end; 200 units reached the maximum speed obtainable. A common feature of all Giulietta models was how well they handled on the road. They provided a combination of sure braking and first-class perform-ance in a spacious sedan. Large production volumes finally forced Alfa to expand its production area and purchase an area covering 2,391,980 square feet (two million square meters) in Arese – eight times larger than the area in Portello.

In Turin, post-war Lancia had to deal with another aggravating circumstance with respect to Alfa – the death of Vincenzo Lancia. They only really recovered with the Aprilia and the Ardea when Arturo Lancia was at the helm of the company. Arturo was Vincenzo's brother and was soon replaced by son Gianni, who had recently obtained his degree in engineering and had a great passion for racing. Francesco De Virgilio, who was in charge of the special research and patents sector, fine-tuned a new V6 60° engine, which was used on another vehicle in 1950. The Aurelia made Lancia and automobile history as an innovation brought about following the Lambda and Aprilia. This new sedan (in production from 1950 to 1958 in versions B10-B21-B15-B22-B12-B20 and B24, in order of debut) changed the nomenclature of Lancia's models, which now used the names of Roman consular roads, and immediately left the Aprilia behind, thanks to its technical features and performance with a V6, 1.8L (1754 cc), 56 hp engine providing maximum spikes up to 84

mph (135 km/h). As for its appearance, the bodywork had uninterrupted sides with no running boards and the now customary pillarless doors. Boano's pencil created the coupe, demonstrating once again the Italian ability to design sporty vehicles that were comfortable for everyday driving. The unforgettable B24 convertible, designed by Pinin Farina, included a Spider version that seduced overseas customers to the extent that the entire production of 240 units ended up in the USA. The evolution of its Convertibile, with a Chevrolet-Corvette style enveloping the windshield and 110 hp engine, made the Aurelia one of the stars of Dino Risi's 1962 film *Il sorpasso* (The Easy Life, aka The Overtaking). This film was a true and realistic cross-section of Italy behind the wheel in those years and portrayed a brilliant Vittorio Gassman launched in a crazy car race from Rome to Viareggio. The 1953 Appia and 1957 Flaminia completed the production of the fifties. The first replaced the Ardea while the second laid the groundwork for future models, which would once

again enchant the world. Refined mechanics – especially the suspensions – and totally new bodywork characterized this large sedan, which, despite avoiding aesthetical dictates from overseas, had a hint of the rear fins and a new radiator grill that broke out of the Lancia moulds at the time. The spacious five-star interior made the Flaminia the official car *par excellence*, to the point that Pinin Farina produced four convertible examples with a long wheelbase for the Quirinal, which are still used today. In addition to the sedan, the Flaminia was also available in Coupe, Convertibile (by Pinin Farina), GT and GTL (by Touring Superleggera) and Sport and Supersport (by Zagato) versions.

168-169 The Lancia Aurelia B20 was the coupe version of the B10 sedan and made its debut in 1951. This elegant vehicle soon became a dream car for the Italian driver due to its captivating shapes, which were combined with interesting performance considering that the six-cylinder 2.0L (1991 cc), 75 hp (subsequently 80 hp) engine allowed it to exceed 99 mph (160 km/h).

169 top This Lancia Flaminia was a classic, luxury sedan, which in addition to demonstrating sober elegance and quality outfitting, also had a long life; it remained in production from 1957 until 1970. Pinin Farina also created four units of the elongated version for the Italian Quirinal.

170 top Jean-Louis Trintignant
and Vittorio Gassman on a
convertible Lancia Aurelia in a
scene from Dino Rossi's 1962
movie Il Sorpasso ('The Easy
Life,' aka 'The Overtaking'). This
film perfectly reflected the
economic boom Italy was
experiencing at the time, based
on consumerism and purchasing
status goods such as the
refrigerator and the automobile.

170-171 The masterpiece
Aurelia, the convertible that
consecrated this Lancia model
on the international scene: It
was the 1954, left-hand drive
B24 Spider (seen here in the S
version) whose panoramic
windshield wrapped around
the sides. The entire production
of 240 units was destined for
the United States.

172 top The unforgettable
Italian actor Marcello Mastroianni
is photographed on a Lancia
Flaminia Convertibile Touring. This
vehicle was manufactured from
1960 to 1964 and, like the
coupe, benefited from many
improvements and innovations
with respect to the sedan,
including an absolute novelty for
Lancia: disk brakes on all four
wheels.

172 bottom The Lancia
Flaminia also lent itself to
Zagato's interpretations, who
appended his stylistic signature
with the 1959 Super Sport
version. It was quite rounded
compared to the versions by
other car designers, especially
the standard truncated tail end.

173 French actress Brigitte
Bardot could not resist the
charm and elegance of the
Lancia Flaminia and was
photographed leaning on the
hood of this Coupe by Pinin
Farina.

The very small Isetta
and the small Bianchina and Amica

Economy cars, city cars, microcars. Call them what you will, compact vehicles with contained operating costs have always sustained automakers, even before the advent of traffic and parking problems. The post-war 1950s needed to offer affordable models that were also reliable, spacious and provided good performance. The theme of bonsai sizes was best expressed by the Isetta, the precursor to the Smart, designed 45 years later. It was 1953 when Renzo Rivolta (a Genoese refrigerator manufacturer and Isothermos industrialist) transferred the Iso company to Bresso in the province of Milan and established Iso Automotoveicoli S.p.A. It created the Isetta, a small vehicle only 7.4 ft (2.27 m) long, with the appearance of the front end of a helicopter. It had two very close rear wheels, or sometimes even a single one, and a 0.2L

(236 cc) engine taken from a motorcycle version, able to transport two passengers and some baggage at 50 mph (80 km/h). It was brilliant considering the times and so innovative that, as was often in the case in Italy, it was not fully understood and had to be taken abroad to seek its fortune. It had good advertising and acclaimed reliability. Seven Isetta vehicles participated in the 1954 Mille Miglia and crossed the finish line at an average speed of 45 mph (72 km/h). At the next edition, four completed the 1000 miles (1600 km) at 49 mph (79 km/h), while truck and light van versions could effortlessly transport two people and had load capacity of 1102 lbs or 500 kg). Despite this, the vehicle to which front-end access was provided through a large door with a side hinge (just as though it were a refrigerator) was not successful in its homeland. But it

174 Showgirl Elena Giusti, behind the wheel of a small Isetta at the 1954 Turin Auto Show, demonstrates the original front end, a large door with a side hinge providing access a small two-seater sofa. The Isetta was a very small vehicle, at only 7.4 feet (2.27 m) and was equipped with an 0.2L (236 cc) motorcycle engine.

was in Germany. Noticed by BMW, which was looking for a model such as this one, the Isetta made its fortune on the German market and sold over 161,000 units between 1955 and 1962 (compared to only 1500 in Italy), including the light van used by the German mail service. The Isetta was also produced under license in France, Spain, Brazil and Great Britain (only the three-wheel version, for economic reasons). The Bianchina was decidedly more fortunate, selling 273,800 units between 1958 and 1969. This elegant city-car, which drew on the mechanics of the Fiat 500, was produced by Autobianchi, a name derived from from Bianchi (bicycles, motorcycles and trucks), which intended to make a comeback in the sector of automobiles. It was able to do so with this company, which also involved Fiat and Pirelli equally. It was 10½ ft (3.23 m) long and offered several styles of body. From the Panoramica, a four-seater sedan, to the Trasformabile, a light van, they all had a distinctive body shape, including that hint of the rear fins that were so well-liked by the public. Finally, its slogan defined it as a "small but very luxurious vehicle." It was friends with Siata, a Turinese company established in 1926 that was characterized by its preparation of Fiat vehicles, which it transformed into small racing cars. The mechanics of the 1949 Amica were taken from the 500B, which drove a compact convertible only 11 ft (3.31 m) long with very sophisticated outfitting and a substantial price-tag (1.5 million Lira; for just 300,000 Lira more, one could purchase the Aurelia). However, this did not prevent it from being moderately successful, especially overseas. Siata also produced a Daina based on the mechanics of the Fiat 1400. This grand touring, coupe or convertible realized by Stabilimenti Farina also met with approval in Italy and abroad.

175 top The qualities of this small city car were indicated on the catwalk. It could climb any slope, drive and park anywhere and used very little gas: one gallon for 62 miles (four liters per 100 km). This picture was taken at the 1954 Turin Auto Show and the vehicle on display is a Mitzi 400, an economy car by Turinese manufacturer Siata.

175 bottom In 1954, Bianchi, Fiat and Pirelli agreed to produce economy cars and the first result was the Bianchina with Fiat 500 mechanics. It was produced from 1958 until 1969 in Trasformabile Special, convertible, Panoramica, Berlina Normale or Special four-seater and Furgoncino versions.

Races with a single (tri)color

Firstly Alfa Romeo and Ferrari. Then Lancia, Maserati, Osca, Cisitalia and Abarth, followed by manufacturer-craftsmen enthusiasts like Stanguellini, Nardi, Moretti and Bandini. Italians had motor racing in their blood and won everything from the post-war period until the end of the 1950s. For proof one need look no further than the roll of honor of the Formula One, Mille Miglia and Targa Florio. The first two editions of the newly created World Championship (started in 1950) were won by Alfa Romeo through Nino Farina and Juan Manuel Fangio on 158 and 159 Alfettas, respectively. In 1952 and 1953 Ascari won with a Ferrari 500, and in 1956 it was the turn of Fangio on a Lancia-Ferrari D50 that Gianni Lancia gave to the Drake together with all the materials for the Formula One when he decided to leave the series. In 1957 Maserati triumphed with Fangio behind the wheel of a 250F, and the year after that Mike Hawthorn won with a Ferrari Dino 246 (the new engine was dedicated to Alfredo Dino Ferrari who had died that year from muscular dystrophy).

176-177 Picture of a thoroughbred: an Alfa Romeo Tipo 159 (better known as the Alfetta), the undisputed protagonist of racing in the 1950s, which led the Milanese manufacturer to win their second Formula One World Championship title in 1951 in addition to the manufacturer's title. This vehicle's list of trophies includes five Grands Prix wins out of eight races, and seven fastest laps.

177 top Giuseppe Farina on an Alfa Romeo 158 crossed the finish line first at the 1950 Europe Grand Prix in Silverstone. He started the race in pole position and also recorded the fastest lap – an excellent encouragement to conquer the Formula One World Championship.

176 top Fine-turning during the 1951 Monza Grand Prix trials: Juan Manuel Fangio's single-seater Alfa Romeo 159. That year, the Argentinean driver won the first of his five Formula One World Championships.

178 and 179 bottom The Grand Prix Maserati 250F was the
Formula One single-seater prepared in 1957 by the Modenese
manufacturer.. After winning the World Championship that year,
Omer Orsi decided to pull the trademark out of Formula One
racing. Today, the 250F is one of the most highly rated single-
seaters with an approximate value of two million Euros.

178-179 Monte Carlo 19 May 1957. Argentinean driver Juan
Manuel Fangio racing a Maserati 250F on the urban circuit at the
Monaco Grand Prix. The Argentinean driver conquered his fifth
world title thanks to the Tridente's single-seater.

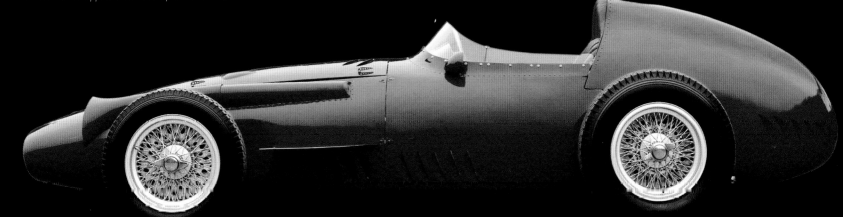

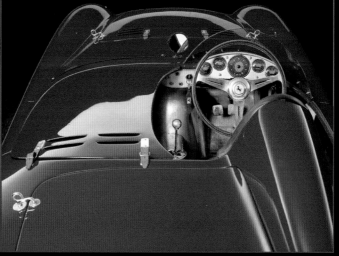

180 top and 180-181 The 1953 Ferrari 500 Mondial was the first red car designed by car designer Sergio Scaglietti for the manufacturer in Maranello and marked the beginning of a long association. Equipped with a four-cylinder engine (a technical choice the Drake was not happy with as he was set on fragmenting the 12 cylinders), this single-seater allowed Ferrari to win often.

181 top Alberto Ascari at the Formula One Italian Grand Prix in Monza in September 1952. The Italian driver won the race in a Formula 2 Ferrari 500 Mondial, with which he also won the championship that same year and the following year.

A look at the Mille Miglia shows how the red cars from Maranello had no rivals from 1949 to 1953. They recorded one victory after another with 166MM, 195S, 340 America, 250S Berlinetta Vignale and 340MM Spider Vignale vehicles and again in 1956 with a 290MM. They also triumphed in the last, tragic edition of 1957, with a 315S, when Marquis De Portago – who always drove with a slipper instead of a shoe on his right foot – caused an accident that cost his life, that of his co-driver and of 10 people in the audience. This accident marked the end of the Mille Miglia. More victories came in the 621 miles (1000 km) in Buenos Aires, the 12 Hours at Sebring and the Targa Florio. Alfa Romeo won the 1947 Mille Miglia and was unbeatable in the races reserved for standard vehicles in which the Giulietta triumphed in Italy, and was only beaten a few times in Europe and the United States by the Porsche 356. After it was transferred to the Orsi family, the Maserati brothers' Bolognese Osca dominated races in the sports car category with a MT4 right from its beginning in 1948 and throughout the 1950s. Oscas won their category in the 12 Hours of Sebring and the 24 Heures du Mans, shining the spotlight on the talent of the Argentinean Alejandro De Tomaso. He had been in Italy since 1955 and in 1959 founded De Tomaso Automobili, which prepared race cars with Osca engines.

182 top The Marzotto-Zignago crew on Ferrari 250 MM Berlinetta no. 556 ready to leave for the 1953 Mille Miglia. Unfortunately, they were forced to withdraw, but a Ferrari would go on to win anyway: Marzotto-Crosara's 340 MM Spider.

182 bottom Vehicles at the starting line of the 1956 12 Hours of Sebring won by Fangio-Castellotti on a Ferrari 860. The drivers walked to their parked vehicles, then turned on the engines and took off on the circuit.

182-183 Joyous arrival in Brescia at the finish line of the 21st edition of the Mille Miglia. The checkered flag is for Alberto Ascari, who won the historic race behind the wheel of a Lancia D24 Carrera Spider.

Ten years earlier, in 1949, it was the turn of the Abarth owned by the Viennese Carlo Abarth. The car and racing enthusiast moved to Italy in 1946 and the following year he brought over materials from Cisitalia (where he had been the company's technical director), which was in economic turmoil, and began the racing cars he prepared. In 1949, the year of his debut, he won 18 races. He then devoted himself to Fiat and Ferrari vehicles, and continued to record victories, even on the international scene,

not to mention the records he set. In the decade from 1956 to 1966 he set 113 international and three world records.

This post-war period was a golden one for Italy and motor racing. Races were held to forget the horrors of the war and they put many fearless racing drivers in the limelight, rich men both in terms of wealth and character — courageous and carefree, but always respectful of each other. They always had the pedal to the metal and often lost their lives in

the process. Clemente Biondetti, Luigi Castellotti, Peter Collins, Marquis De Portago, Luigi Musso and Achille Varzi are the names that the world of racing sacrificed in this period alone. Nuvolari himself eventually died in bed after a serious illness in 1953. He continued racing as long as he could and was only able to forget all of his real life's disappointments and sorrows when he was behind the steering wheel when he won and lived his thrilling sport-loving life.

184 top Everything was in place on the Monza Circuit in 1956 to see this vehicle, the Fiat Abarth Enduro, and its extremely aerodynamic torpedo-shaped body challenge speed.

184-185 The mechanical specifications of the 1962 Fiat Abarth 1000 were taken from the Fiat 600 D, but it was equipped with a 66 hp engine. The last version, in 1969, had a radial cylinder head developed 112 hp engine, allowing it to reach 124 mph (200 km/h).

CHAPTER 5

From the Dolce
Vita of the 60s
to the crisis
in the 70s

The automobile was perfected, was for the masses ... and became stuck in traffic!

The 1960s and 1970s began with the automobile, launched by an economic boom that involved everything and everyone from 1958 to 1964. The automobiles of this age had modern shapes, were status symbols for the middle class and *divertissements* for the more affluent. The car became a mass means of transport that nobody was prepared to renounce. Accomplice to this was large-scale industrialized mass production, which reduced production costs and, consequently, the final price. The car even became affordable for the poorer classes and a symbol of prosperity like the television or washing machine. Sales skyrocketed as a result. Just think that, in 1960, the Italian market numbered 381,385 motor vehicles, compared to 1,397,039 in 1979 (source: UNRAE). In 1965, when the number of vehicles in circulation outnumbered scooters and motorcycles compared to the previous year, there was one car for every nine inhabitants. Twenty years later that number was one car for every three people, and in excess of 20 million vehicles were circulating in Italy. It was still the 1960s when Italy was finally able to keep up with the growth of the automobile in the other industrialized countries and started witnessing a uniform diffusion of cars across northern and southern

Italy. More than half the cars were small (under 0.8L or 800 cc). In the 1970s, manufacturers started taking an interest in youth, survivors of the student protests that had culminated in 1968 and who became a new market to conquer. From a social perspective, the car was linked to mass tourism, as the average Italian used it mainly to go to the beach on vacation. There were two negative consequences of this mass motorization – traffic and pollution – problems that continue today and that we know will continue in the future. City centers became jammed. In Milan, Rome and Naples and in the other important cities, people sat in lines during rush hour and even on highways to go on vacation in August when the factories closed for the month. Bypasses, beltways and slip roads, together with the parking lots that were built, were insufficient before they were even completed. Basically, nothing had changed. From an environmental perspective, the first legislation on the subject of pollution dates back to 1966 and specified that motor vehicles must not produce pollutants, the opaque smoke from diesel-operated models must not exceed the limits detailed by the regulation, and periodic servicing must also include checking emissions. A European directive was laid down in 1971, but this was disregarded in Italy. Precise legislation to apply and enforce was lacking for the entire decade

because the administrations and manufacturers underestimated the problem. In the sixties and seventies, manufacturers were committed to competing through technology, a challenge based on innovation that Italians fought with their heads held high and with tools equal to those of the rest of the world, while also being able to count on more subtle elements, such as elegance and an innate sense of taste. The car had reached maturity, it just needed to be perfected. During the sixties, the alternator took the place of the generator, luxury models were equipped with power steering and front-wheel drive became the norm after its national debut on the Lancia Flavia. This vehicle also mounted a four-cylinder engine contrasted by silent running and no vibrations assembled transversally at the front of the car, just like today's widespread layout (a scheme that was introduced by Fiat through Autobianchi on the Primula). Injection began appearing in the place of carburetors, but it was mechanical and still required years of fine-tuning before it became electronic towards the end of the seventies and the beginning of the eighties, when this innovation distorted all automobile equilibriums. It had become necessary to deal with the problem of pollution, as it provided precise fuel supply and ignition, which resulted in reduced emissions and wasted energy. This theme reached its climax with the oil crisis in 1973, which caused the price of gas to skyrocket and led to austerity, license plate restrictions and 'Sundays on foot.'

186-187 *This 220 hp 1964 Ferrari 250 GT luxury coupe reached 149 mph (240 km/h) and was just one of the many variations of this elegant grand touring vehicle.*

188 *A scene from Federico Fellini's 1960 movie La dolce vita (The Sweet Life). Marcello Mastroianni and Anita Ekberg on an Alfa*

Romeo Giulietta are struggling with the paparazzi.

189 *The automobile increasingly became the protagonist in movies, as demonstrated by this shot from Vittorio De Sica's 1963 movie Ieri, oggi e domani (Yesterday, Today and Tomorrow), starring Sofia Loren and Marcello Mastroianni, the two passengers in the front.*

190 top The Lancia Fulvia made its debut in 1963 at the Geneva Auto Show and replaced the glorious Appia. This was another masterpiece by the Turinese manufacturer, a spacious sedan with square, sharp lines that were decidedly original for the times.

190-191 The 1974 Safari, one of the last variations of the super lucky Lancia Fulvia Coupe third series sports car that dominated in rallies. Only 900 numbered units were made, with simplified outfitting.

Lancia looked forwards – with its drive

By now, the world was accustomed to the surprises that the car manufacturing company, founded by Vincenzo Lancia, threw at it. Lancia's ability to evolve the automobile and create models whose style and technology broke the mould remained intact for decades, including the 1960s. The popular Flavia introduced front-wheel drive and was the first car in Italy to feature disk brakes. Then there was the boxer engine, that is, with opposed cylinders, and first a 1.5L (1500 cc), 78 hp engine and then, considering it was a little undersized and therefore had poor performance and consumption, the 1.8L (1800 cc), 92 hp engine, which became 102 hp in 1965 thanks to the injection system. As always, the sedan was flanked by Pininfarina's Coupe, Vignale's Convertibile

and Zagato's Sport version, the latter having a unique design true to the car designer's heritage. It was characterized as a three-seater coupe (in aluminum) with a front end that extended past the angled, protruding radiator grill with respect to the recessed lights, making it as aerodynamic as possible.

These were also the years of the new factory in Chivasso, close to Turin (still active today), of the Lancia family equity stake being sold to industrialist Cesare Pesente, of the eclectic and nonconformist engineer Antonio Fessia, who started with the company in 1955 and used the Flavia as inspiration for a series of creations worthy of its iconic progenitors Lambda, Aprilia and Aurelia. So the Fulvia was called upon to replace the Appia with a four-cylinder, narrow V (13°), 1.1L (1092 cc) engine tilted 45° to the left. This was a great masterpiece of motor engineering developed on a low-powered engine. In 1965, the Fulvia Coupe enchanted drivers both on the roads and the race tracks and started the automaker's tradition of international supremacy in this discipline, which continued through the 1990s. Versions included the Rallye, Rallte HF and Montecarlo (without bumpers and with a black hood), and also the HF, which stood for High Fidelity. The 1.6L (1600 cc), created for competition, made history known as the *fanalona* or large headlight; its light units included auxiliary headlights, necessary during night-time racing. These 11 years brought great satisfaction to Lancia. It ended Fulvia's lifecycle in 1976 by re-launching the second generation of the Flavia with new bodywork, while retaining the same style. In 1971 it was the turn of the 2000 and its Coupe version; this was an evolution of the Flavia 2000, but with more substantial changes to the appearance of its front and tail ends, while its mechanics remained much the same with respect to the model from which it was drawn. The next year saw the debut of Lancia's new lifecycle. The Beta was in fact the first tangible result of Lancia's transfer to Fiat in 1969. In keeping with the brand's tradition, it again took its name from the Greek alphabet, and was available as a hatchback and in engine sizes of 1.4L, 1.6L and 1.8L (1400 cc, 1600 cc and 1800 cc) from Fiat. The goal was to double sales with new models that were able

to maintain the brand's innovative features from the sixties. As always, the Beta included a coupe, Pininfarina designed the Spider (assembled by Zagato) and the Montecarlo, while the 1975 HPE (High Performance Estate) stood out from the pack. It was a three-door, high performance coupe station wagon with a fifties-style radiator grill. The final year of the 1970s was a year for restyling in terms of appearance (the radiator grill became the same for all vehicles and the 'family' concept was introduced so that a brand could immediately be identified), of outfitting (the dashboard had been given the nickname *Gruyère* due to the numerous holes for indicators and a considerable number of warning lights), and of mechanics, with the introduction of electronic ignition. Finally, it was the turn of the third and final generation, in 1980. The Trevi sedan, equipped with a 1.3L, 1.6L or 2.0L (1300 cc, 1600 cc or 2000 cc) carburetor or injection engine and the supercharged Volumex, with its positive displacement compressor, were introduced. During the Beta years, a model was developed in 1973 on the chassis of the Fulvia 1.6 HF, which yet again focused the spotlight on the world of the automobile, both for its road-legal and race versions: the Stratos. This fascinating coupe, with a futuristic, wedge-shaped profile, was called on to replace the Fulvia HF1.6 in long distance races and was equipped with a Dino Ferrari V6, 2.4L (2418 cc) engine. Its aerodynamic profile, supertested chassis group and sophisticated mechanics made it unbeatable in rallies and unforgettable for fans. Within the realm of the coupe, the Gamma coupe was an elegant, square sedan designed by Pininfarina that followed the trend of the high-end hatchback. Unfortunately, it emerged during an unhappy period as the oil crisis was still not completely over by 1976.

Three years later it was the turn of a model that re-launched sales and put Lancia's accounts back in order: the compact Delta. As suggested by Giugiaro, it was derived from the Fiat Ritmo and had the period's trendy square, extended profiles, a back tailgate, a little less room in the back, and mechanics that had a lot in common with the Beta. The Delta had chrome plating, enveloping resin bumpers, a sophisticated dashboard and was outfitted to match the brand's level, all of which made this vehicle the success of the 1980s and helped it win the Car of the Year award in 1980.

192 and 193 The Lancia Delta made its debut in 1979 and was the model that re-launched the Turinese brand both in terms of sales and image, considering that the previous models were not up to the brand's standards of prestige and innovation. Designed by Giorgetto Giugiaro, it immediately conquered the public with its square, sharp shapes that pleased just as much as the large back tailgate and detailed interior outfitting. And its road performance was valid too, thanks to its agility and ease of handling. The first units were equipped with 1.3L and 1.5L (1300 cc and 1500 cc) engines and then with a 1.6L (1600 cc) engine and then the first of the turbocharged versions, which dominated World Championship rallies over the years.

LANCIA DELTA

LANCIA DELTA

The sixties and seventies were complex but not complicated for Ferrari. The distinction between the production of road-legal models and race models, which in turn was a separate sector from Formula One, became more apparent. Marking this division was one of the three iconic models of the period, the 250 GTO, a hands-down winner in GT races but whose comfortable urban road use required owners to make significant changes in terms of soundproofing and waterproofing. The captivating and marvelous shapes of the 1962 GTO were the work of Sergio Scaglietti, who relied on his expertise and kept drawings in his head and not on paper. He started with a 250 GT Berlinetta with a lower engine and transmission and close-fitting bodywork, which explains the roundness of the fenders and engine compartment.

Young Mauro Forghieri (who was given the project after replacing Marcello Gandini, who left Maranello following a quarrel with Giotto Bizzarrini's group) had the task of giving the vehicle those excellent road qualities that had made it the king of the races. The debut by the GTO obscured other models, such as the flagship 400 Superamerica (1960) and its successor, the 500 Superfast (1964), the 330 GT 2+2 (1964), flanked two years later by the 330 (GTC, GTS, GT California), both of which were replaced by the 365 (GTC, GTS and GT 2+2) in 1968, which brought with them the injection system, and the 275 (1964) and its versions GTB-GTS-GTB/4 and GTS/4 (the 4 stands for four camshafts rather than two).

194-195 The Ferrari 275 Gtb made its debut in 1964 replacing the 250 Gtl. Designed by Pininfarina and built by Scaglietti, it was equipped with a V12 3.3L (3285 cc), 280 hp engine that reached 148 mph (238 km/h). Numerous versions were manufactured, including the 250 Tour de France, Swb, Gto followed by the second series starting in 1965 with an extended wheelbase. This series included the Gtb/4 with four camshafts (instead of two) and the Spider Gts.

196 Worker working on a 250 GTO in 1962 in the historic Ferrari factory in Maranello in the province of Modena. Two years earlier, the business name had changed from Auto Costruzioni Ferrari to Sefac (Societa' esercizio fabbriche automobile e corse), the plant had expanded and the assembly lines had been modernized and optimized to allow 500 automobiles to be manufactured each year.

196-197 The 1962 Ferrari 250 GTO in a unique, elegant silver color, is one of the icons of Ferrari production. It has always been sought after by international collectors and can reach exorbitant prices considering that only a total of 36 units were manufactured until 1964. The O stands for omologato, or type-approved, and the car was the result of a 250 Gt racing coupe with a modified chassis. It was equipped with a V12 3.0L (2953 cc), 290 hp engine that reached 171 mph (280 km/h). It was fascinating, super fast and thrilling, both on the road and track.

198-199 Dino identified Ferraris with a six-cylinder engine. The versions' first two numbers indicate the displacement, and the third refers to the number of cylinders. This was the first 1968 206Gt, followed by the 246 Gt and Gts Spider. A total of 2487 units were manufactured by 1974. The engine was placed centrally and in later versions was 2.4L (2418 cc) with 195 hp.

The 1968 Dino coupe (a separate brand for six-cylinder vehicles that gained its name from the son who died prematurely) was followed by the 246, including an open sports-car version, and the 1969 365, better known as the Daytona after its success on the famous American circuit two years prior, all led to important stages in Ferrari's evolution, both in terms of mechanics and style. The Dino's engine was moved back to a central or rear transversal position, furthering the trend started for the Formula One ve-hicles, which Ferrari actually believed was more diffi-cult for road-legal vehicles. In fact, the Drake main-tained that the oxen (that is the engine) had to be in front of the wagon (the car) and not the other way around. History and future models would prove him wrong in this regard. This was a future that Ferrari preferred to guarantee for his company in another, more concrete fashion considering that, on June 21, 1969, Fiat took over 50 percent of Ferrari, but left complete independence to the Drake to manage the racing side of things. The Daytona had more extend-ed forms with a wedge-shaped front end and Per-spex insert (a type of Plexiglas) that housed light units and replaced the roundness and curved profiles used to that point. It was almost a stylistic necessity, considering that its competitors, the Maserati Ghibli and the Lamborghini Miura, were headed in this di-rection. However, the versions intended for the Unit-ed States implemented retractable lights, a solution that later became standard on subsequent models.

200 The Ferrari 308 GTB was presented at the Paris Auto Show in 1975 and replaced the Dino. Designed by Pininfarina and produced by Scaglietti, it was manufactured in fiberglass until early 1977. Low, wide and very sporty with front pop-up headlamps, it was equipped with a very expensive bearing chassis with lattice pipe framework and a rear V8 2.9L (2926 cc), 250 hp engine that was capable of reaching 157 mph (252 km/h). It was also manufactured in a Gts Spider version and, starting in 1980, with a 2.0L engine, including a supercharged version (208 Gtb, Gts and Turbo).

200-201 The Ferrari 512BB made its debut in 1976, having evolved from the 365 Gt4Bb. Its wedge-shaped front end and powerful lines combined to produce the superlative performance of this 12-cylinder, 4.9L (4942 cc), 360 hp engine that reached 174 mph (280 km/h) with suitable comfort and on-road silence. The injection version made its debut in 1981 and was replaced in 1984 by the Testarossa, which, unlike this model, could also be exported to the United States because it complied with overseas type-approval legislation.

If the Daytona housed its powerful 12-cylinder, V 352 hp engine 'in front of the cart,' the 1973 365 GT4BB was a demonstration of power and drivability, ready to challenge Lamborghini and Maserati. It was the first vehicle to present a Ferrari 12-cylinder boxer engine at the tail end of the vehicle. The 365 also included the GT4 2+2, the largest Ferrari by Pininfarina, with the task of comfortably seating two passengers in the back, while Bertone had the job of developing a more affordable Ferrari with the Dino-branded 308 GT4. Created in 1973, the vehicle was equipped with a V8, 3.0L (3000 cc) engine (a 208 version was equipped with a 2.0L (2000 cc) engine

exclusively for the Italian market to benefit from lower taxation). The new 1975 308 GTB (Gran Turismo Berlinetta) was the result of work by Pininfarina. Low, wide, sinewy and sinuous, it oozed horsepower (225) and determination (158 mph or 255 km/h), not to mention those pop-up headlamps. This sporting experience for two made its debut with fiberglass bodywork by Scaglietti, then 1976 saw the turn of the versions with sheet-steel bodywork, and the Spider came out the year after. It remained on the market until 1985, starred in the TV series Magnum PI and ended its lifecycle with the 2.0L (2000 cc) 208 GTB and GTS versions and a special 308 GTBqv

with four-valve cylinder heads and electronic injection. There were also innovations for the 1976 400 GT, the first Ferrari with an automatic transmission (by GM) while an iconic model – the 512 BB, in production from 1976 to 1984, including an injection version – ended the 1970s. The 512 BB evolved from the 365 GT4BB, and was designed by Pininfarina and built by Scaglietti, with 1936 units being produced in total. It stood out for its fairing, ultra-sloping hood, pantograph windshield wipers and tail end with six-element light units and just as many exhaust manifolds. It was, naturally, a high-performance car: its 360 hp allowed it to reach 174 mph (280 km/h).

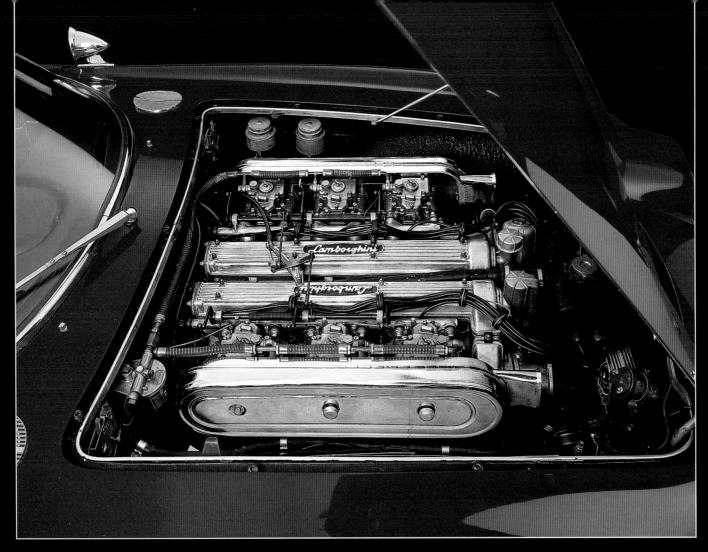

202 top The engine compartment of the Lamborghini 350 Gt provided a peak at its 12-cylinder, 3.5L (3464 cc), 280 hp engine allowing the vehicle, produced by the manufacturer in Sant'Agata Bolognese, to reach 155 mph (250 km/h).

202-203 The 350 Gt was the first Lamborghini and made its debut in 1964 as an alternative to Ferrari and Maserati. Initially only 13 units were manufactured, with a unique line and strong personality that pleased both the public and those responsible for the work. It remained in production until 1966.

Miura, Countach, Espada: Lamborghini astonished the world

From its beginning to its bankruptcy, reaching the peaks of automobile excellence in between, and all in 10 years. Lamborghini would not have even existed without Enzo Ferrari and his difficult nature. The manufacturing company from Sant'Agata Bolognese was founded based on the revenge sought by Ferruccio Lamborghini, an industrialist with a passion for engines whose business had been in tractors. One day, when he complained to the Drake about his new Ferrari's clutch and tried to give him advice on how to improve it, he was told, "You continue building tractors and let me build my sports cars." Ferruccio wanted to prove he could produce better vehicles than those built in Maranello, and made a half a billion Lira available to build cars *with the balls of a bull.* In today's money, this budget could be compared with that of modern oil magnates who purchase soccer teams and have almost unlimited budgets for buying players. And so Lamborghini recruited Giotto Bizzarrini (formerly with Ferrari), Gianpaolo Dallara, Paolo Stanziani and many technicians from the *Prancing Stallion* to create a 350

hp GT in his new, flaming factory in Sant'Agata Bolognese.

The 350 GT with 10 extra hp was created in just six months. Its purebred sporty shapes and rear axle with independent wheels (while his competitors were still assembling a rigid rear axle) captivated everyone at its presentation to the press in October 1963. Ferrari and Maserati were informed and were forced to acknowledge the force of the new competitor in 1966. An un-

known, Marcello Gandini, had replaced Giorgetto Giugiaro at Bertone, and hit the headlines for having created the Miura, a sports car years ahead of its time in terms of style, and still tremendously fashionable 40 years later. The name was taken from a breed of bulls (Ferruccio Lamborghini was a Taurus and his trademark was a bull) and the performance created by the V12 4.0L (3929 cc), 350 hp engine can be summed up in its maximum speed of 186 mph (300 km/h).

203 top Lamborghini mechanics in Sant'Agata Bolognese in October 1965 at work on the chassis of what would be the company's masterpiece and icon: Bertone's P400 Miura.

204-205 Automobile enthusiasts have no choice but to bow down to this vehicle. It is the classic orange Lamborghini Miura, equipped with standard front headlamps "with eyelashes." It was Bertone's masterpiece: The car got its name from a ferocious breed of fighting bulls and made its debut in 1966. It was able to reach 186 mph (300 km/h). It was manufactured until 1968, including the 385 hp Sv version, the S being an example of a Roadster.

The 1968 Espada, originating from the Marzial prototype (also by Gandini), was even more futuristic. Low and long, with an extended hood and majestic tail end, it didn't have its precursor's beetle-wing doors but still had a revolutionary style because it favored rounded profiles as compared to the mandatory wedge shapes of the time. This was the same wedge shape that became central again in the 1971 Countach (a Piedmont word meaning astonishment), a wild but road-legal racing car with a multi-tubular structure and the engine located in front of the rear axle, with a central transmission, six twin-barrel carburetors, and 375 hp able to reach speeds up to 196 mph (315 km/h). There was also room for the Urraco and a calmer, more affordable Lambo (Lamborghini's nickname) that had its siblings' stylistic elements that were famous for facing the difficulties of the oil crisis. However, it only started being delivered in 1974 due to technical problems. This crisis took hold of the manufacturer from Sant'Agata and forced Ferruccio Lamborghini to sell 51 percent of the company to Swiss Rossetti and then, three years later in 1971, sell the remaining 49 percent to engineering industrialist René Leimer. Bankruptcy befell the company in 1980, despite new capital, but new life returned over the next decade.

206 top   The Lamborghini Marzial was a futuristic concept car designed by Marcello Gandini in 1967 on behalf of the Bertone design studio. This prototype made its debut at the London Auto Show that year.

206-207   The Lamborghini Countach made its debut in 1971. This time its name originated from a typical Piedmont expression of astonishment. The supercar's wedge-shaped design was typical of the period, the 375-hp engine was in front of the rear axle, was equipped with a central transmission and reached a maximum speed of 196 mph (315 km/h).

207 top Another masterpiece from the father of the Miura, the Lamborghini Urraco. Named after the bull that killed the famous bullfighter Manolete, the Urraco was designed by Marcello Gandini during his years of collaboration with the Bertone Studio.

De Tomaso, Maserati, Asa and Iso sports cars – what passion!

Italy was a breeding ground of sport-car automakers during the sixties and seventies, and not just Ferrari, Lamborghini and Alfa Romeo. Take for example Argentinean Alejandro De Tomaso who, having established the company that bore his name in Modena in 1959 to prepare race cars with Osca engines, decided to build his own cars. The Vallelunga made its debut in 1965, and was first built by Fissore and then by Ghia, a car designer who, together with Vignale, was taken on by De Tomaso in 1967 and by Ford in 1972.

The Vallelunga was so interesting in terms of style that it was chosen for exhibition at New York's Museum of Modern Art (MOMA), but it didn't disappoint on the road either and earned the nickname of the Italian Lotus. Its 1.5L (1500 cc), 105-135 hp Ford engine reached 134 mph (215 km/h). The Pantera from the 1970s was the jewel in De Tomaso's crown. It was created in 1970 after the automaker became a part of Ford's sphere and was presented with a central, eight-cylinder engine by the Detroit manufacturer. Other models included the 1970 Deauville and the Longchamp 2+2 in 1972, the year the factory in Modena was closed, and Alejandro left his company only to take it over again in 1976. The Pantera completed its lifecycle in 1995.

208 De Tomaso was the equivalent of Pantera, the 1968 super sports car with a central V8, 330 hp engine that could reach 162 mph (260 km/h) produced in the former factories of Carrozzeria Vignale in Turin, which had been taken over by Alejandro De Tomaso after an agreement with Ford.

208-209 *The first road-legal vehicle produced by De Tomaso in Modena was the Vallelunga, with a central Ford engine, fiberglass body and unique tubular bearing chassis for the gearbox and transmission. First assembled by Fissore and then by Ghia, it was selected by New York's MOMA and described as the Italian Lotus.*

The Sebring also made its debut on Maserati grounds in Modena in the sixties. It took up the 3500 GT engine again but was given a new, successful look thanks to Michelotti who was working for Vignale. Three years later it was the turn of the Mistral and Quattroporte. The first was a very successful, compact coupe with excellent sales results. The second started the epic journey of the large company car whose name is still used. When it made its debut, it was the fastest flagship in the world, reaching 143 mph (230 km/h). It provided comfort and absolute

luxury without compromising on-road performance. Still not satisfied, a decision was made at Maserati in 1965 to flank it with an even more powerful version, recognized for its double headlights, with a V8 engine that increased from 4.2L to 4.7L (4200 cc to 4700 cc.). The next year was the turn of the Mexico and Ghibli by Giugiaro, an example of style and elegance applied to a sports car. French air blew into Modena in 1968, as the Orsi family sold out to Citröen, which kept Maserati until 1973. It produced the Indy with a front engine, the Bora, Merak, Khamsin with a central

engine as requested by the market at that time, and the second generation of the Quattroporte, equipped with the French manufacturer's sophisticated hydropneumatic suspension. In 1975 ownership was transferred to Benelli, owned by Alejandro De Tomaso, after a two-year period of administration by Gepi, an institution that helped companies in economic crisis. The Kyalami coupe and Quattroporte III, designed by Giugiaro who gave it unique class and prestige, were the first results of the Argentinean's management at the end of the 1970s.

210-211 This was one of the masterpieces of Giorgetto Giugiaro, who was working for Ghia in 1966. It is the Maserati Ghibli (here in the Spider version manufactured from 1969 to 1973). Beautiful, elegant and powerful, this convertible two-seater was capable of reaching 180 mph (290 km/h).

211 top This model was named after a wind. The Maserati Bora made its debut in 1971 and was the trademark's first vehicle with a central engine. A very fast grand touring, it had 310 hp and reached 174 mph (280 km/h).

Coupé G.L. *Iso Grifo*
2 posti

IL NUOVO GIOIELLO DELL'AUTOMOBILI

212-213 and 212 top Just like the playbill above says, the Iso Grifo was the new Italian automobile jewel. It made its debut in 1963 and was a super-fast Gt, as was common at the time. It was created as a result of collaboration by personalities including Giorgetto Giugiaro, who designed the bodywork, and Giotto Bizzarrino and Renzo Rivolta, *the founder of the Milanese brand. Highly regarded in America and able (in any version) to reach 186 mph (300 km/h), it was often equipped with Made in USA engines by Chevrolet or Ford, like the one shown here from the second series in 1974. This was the second-last year of production, not only of the Grifo but of any Iso.*

Iso also started thinking about sports models and radically changed direction after the Isetta. The Rivolta GT300 made its debut in 1962. It was a sophisticated four-seater GT, designed by Giugiaro and assembled by Bertone, and was equipped with the Chevrolet Corvette's V8, 5.3L (5300 cc), 300 hp engine and became quite successful overseas when combined with the 340 hp GT340 version. Pleased with the results, Renzo Rivolta thought big and wanted a sports car that was able to reach 186 mph (300 km/h). Bertone designed the profiles and engineer Giotto Bizzarrini pulled the Grifo out of the small Milanese automaker's top hat. It had a Chevrolet 405 hp engine and various versions (Lusso, Competizione plus a less powerful 365 hp version and two more powerful 5.0L (5000 cc) and 7.0L (7000 cc) versions). In 1973, thought was even given to entering Formula One, but despite fresh American capital, the crisis strangled the company and it closed down in 1975.

Ferrari was behind the Asa 1000GT, which was immediately called the Ferrarina and ordered from Bertone by the Drake himself. It was a compact coupe, equipped with a 1.0L (1000 cc) engine, with a chassis taken from the Ferrari 250 GT and outfitted like a high-end car. It was successfully displayed at the 1961 Turin Auto Show, however production only started the following year when Milanese industrialist Oronzio De Nora and his son made an agreement with Ferrari to purchase the projects and patents to manufacture it. It finally made its debut in 1964, after the creation of the Spider version (the body of the production model would be in fiberglass) and the 1000GTC prototype with a central engine. The first one was delivered to ship magnate Achille Lauro. Despite other versions that had more powerful engines and even a coupe-open sports car designed for the US market, the Asa was not as successful as expected and high production costs (which exceeded its sale price) forced production to be interrupted in 1966.

A swarm of low-powered, high-performing sports cars were decidedly more affordable, such as those created by Abarth and Giannini with Fiat internals and whose race victories attracted an audience of young enthusiasts. Standing out among them were Abarth's 500 and 595 versions originating from the Fiat 500, such as the Giannini 500 TV (Turismo Veloce), able to squeeze up to 32 hp (compared to the standard version's 13 hp) out of the Turinese microcar, or the iconic A112 Abarth 58 hp, the high-performance version of the Autobianchi A1112.

214 top Carlo Abarth created one of his best and most famous elaborations based on a Fiat 500 by transforming the pleasant economy car into a mini racing car able to excite both on the road and the track.

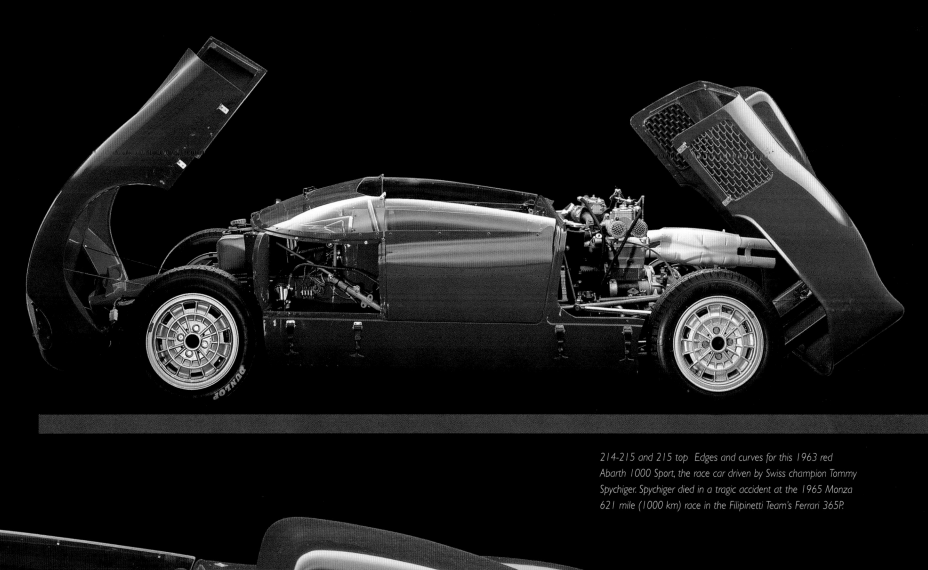

214-215 and 215 top Edges and curves for this 1963 red
Abarth 1000 Sport, the race car driven by Swiss champion Tommy
Spychiger. Spychiger died in a tragic accident at the 1965 Monza
621 mile (1000 km) race in the Filipinetti Team's Ferrari 365P.

Alfa Romeo always on the racetrack

216-217 *The Alfa Romeo Giulietta Spring Gt made its debut in 1963, a four-seater coupe designed by Bertone. Its mechanics were those of the powerful sedan, the Giulia Ti, with two additional twin-barrel carburetors and disk brakes for an everyday sports car.*

Giulia, Giulietta, Duetto, 33 Stradale, Alfetta and Alfasud: these were the Milanese automaker's leading models, known to more or less everyone, even those who knew very little about cars. They all had that sports personality and performance originating from races, where the *Biscione*'s trademark excelled. One need only think of the Giulia TZ (Tubolare Zagato) in the international races of its category, in which it was the car to beat, or the 33 that won the World Sports Prototype Championship, or its return to Formula One in 1977 by first providing the engine for the Brabham and then in 1980, with its own vehicle and its first two victories with the 158 and 159 Alfetta. The name Alfetta was brought back for this sedan (and later GT, GTV and Turbodelta) in 1972, resulting in successful sales and becoming the first Italian turbo diesel in 1979. There was also the super fast Giulia adopted by the Italian police force, and criminals. It made its debut in 1962 and also provided solutions in terms of safety, such as the programmed-deformation body in the event of an accident, a strengthened driver and passenger compartment to protect the occupants, set-back steering box and safety belt preset. The Giulia had something for everyone, with TI (Turismo Internazionale), Super, Sprint, Sprint GT and GTA, TZ, TZ2 and Spider versions and 1.3L (1300 cc) and 1.6L (1600 cc) engines in various configurations. Performance enthusiasts found the Giulia to be the ideal vehicle, despite some details that required fine tuning, such as the gears at the steering wheel, and the three-seater front bench. In 1964, in response to these criticisms Alfa proposed the option of a gearshift and separate front seats. The TZ models led to the birth of the Autodelta by engineer Carlo Chiti (an unforgettable figure for Alfa Romeo) and Ludovico Chizzola (dealer for the automaker in Udine), who prepared the vehicles for races. They were so successful that they became the official race team for the brand and made a true, well deserved comeback to the world of racing (Alfa stopped participating with Fangio's 159).

The sixties and seventies were also a period in which the Milanese automaker looked to the southern part of Italy and, in order to favor work there, decided to make use of the area of Pomigliano d'Arco in the province of Naples. The Alfasud was created there in 1972, which led to total production capacity and the employment of 15,000 workers.

All this in fact halted expansion in Arese and

Portello and the crisis resulted in difficult times. Despite this, models like the 2000 and the Montreal (a beautiful 2+2 coupe, with a V8 engine, that evolved from the 1968 1750) in 1971 and the Giulietta in 1977 (the heir to the Alfetta) were created, while other gems were not forgotten, such as the Duetto. The name was decided on the basis of a competition held by Alfa to name the 1600 Spider, but could not be officially adopted

because it was already copyrighted for a cookie. The Duetto was also known as the cuttlebone for its analogous shape, and in the United States as The Graduate, after its great success in the film of the same name starring Dustin Hoffman (in Italy, the name of the film was *Il laureato*). The Duetto was a timeless vehicle, so much so that it stayed in production with various updates until 1995.

On the other hand, the road-legal 33 version

218-219 The Alfa Romeo 1600 Spider was better known as the Osso di sepia (cuttlebone) due to the shape of the body, or as the Duetto, thanks to the results of a referendum promoted by the Milanese brand to give the vehicle its name. That name was then never used because it was already registered by the Pavesi company, for a biscuit. The 1600 Spider was the sporty

convertible for youngsters in the late 60s. It made its debut in 1966 and was produced in various versions until 1995.

219 top Mike Nichols' 1967 movie The Graduate, starring Katherine Ross and Dustin Hoffman, consecrated the Alfa Romeo Duetto in the United States to such an extent that the sports car took the same name as the movie.

expectedly oozed racing. This iconic vehicle, whose heart and soul were sporty and whose appearance remains highly regarded, was the result of work by the eclectic Franco Scaglione and Autodelta. Its aerodynamic shape, with a 2.0L (2000 cc), 230 hp engine and extremely high engine speed (8800 rpm) enabled it to reach a maximum speed of 128 mph (206 km/h), 95 percent of the performance obtained with the race model.

Fiat took all:
Autobianchi, Lancia,
Ferrari and Abarth

This 20-year period confirmed Fiat's different pace compared to the other Italian automakers. Its large size and leading role in the country's economic and social fabric drove it to process different strategies that crossed national borders. This practice of looking abroad was concretized in agreements such as the one with the Soviet Union in 1966 for the factory in Togliattigrad that was able to produce 2000 124 Zigulì a day, and was further boosted with the arrival of as Fiat chairman of Gianni Agnelli (the grandson of Giovanni and son of Edoardo, who died in 1935). So how did Fiat achieve international growth but also continuous internal expansion? With the acquisition of Abarth, Autobianchi, 50 percent of Ferrari (at the time) and Lancia, which led to the establishment in 1979 of Fiat Auto S.p.A. It grouped together these brands, plus Innocenti in 1984, Alfa Romeo in 1986 and a stake in Ferrari that increased to 90 percent in 1991, three years after the death of the Drake. What is certain is that only Fiat could offer an almost complete range of vehicles, which was the object of continuous renewal with models known to everyone (at least one of which was owned by every the family). The range also included the 500, which had become the D (starting in 1960) and was more of an automobile (including more detailed comforts such as windshield washers and a back bench truly for two), the F (starting in 1965) that stood out for its suicide door, the more luxurious L in 1968 and finally the R from 1972 to 1975. Acronyms aside, and keeping in mind that the Giardiniera station wagon was also in the range, the 500 was and remained a four-wheel icon and a funda-

mental example of a city car because it was a vehicle that everyone liked and needed. Today we would describe it as transversal and targetless. In addition, Fiat continued to confirm its specialization in small cars, although the range had something to please all tastes and sizes. The 124 was created in 1966 to replace the unforgettable 1300-1500 (the renewed 1100R resisted until 1969 and was then replaced by the 128). It was a comfortable, square, four-door sedan with a new, solid and affordable 1.2L (1200 cc), 60 hp engine. And the well built Spider – the antagonist of the Duetto Alfa, Coupe, Familiare, Special

and T – was a global success. One and a half million units were sold in Italy and four million world-wide, not only as a result of the Fiat-USSR agreement but also because when it was replaced by the 131 in 1974, it continued to be manufactured in Russia, but also in Africa (South Africa and Morocco), South-America, Malaysia, Turkey, Bulgaria, Spain, Portugal, Yugoslavia and Ireland. The 1967 125 drew on the 124 but was more detailed and sporty and was well received by the general public. Another million-selling vehicle was the 1964 850, presented with more power and increased comfort to expand the offer

that already included superstar models such as the 500 and 600. It had a rear 0.8L (850 cc), 34 hp engine, two doors and room for five. The 850 was the fastback precursor to the Familiare, which originated from the Multipla, and was presented as a small, light van with the functionality of a modern four-door, seven-seater minivan with three rows (2+3+3). It was also the forerunner to the streamlined Coupe 2+2 and Spider by Bertone, which in the United States was given the nickname Little Ferrari and was replaced in 1972 by the original X1/9 (also by the Turinese car designer).

The 850 underwent some restyling in 1968 before re-emerging as the Special, Sport Coupe and Sport Spider. These were modest sports cars compared with the Dino Spider and Coupe (1966-1967), which were created based on an agreement with Ferrari (in fact, the 850 opened the way to Fiat's participation in the *Prancing stallion*) to use the Dino six-cylinder engine, and allowed Fiat to collaborate with Pininfarina. The seventies had a swarm of models, including the prestigious flagship 130 with its fascinating square shape (Agnelli even ordered a special dark blue one), the sedan Coupe by Pininfarina, and the 1969 128, Fiat's first front-wheel drive with a transversal, 1.1L (1110 cc) engine, a great road model with exceptional road qualities and very spacious, thanks to the absence of the transmission tunnel. It was also produced in Familiare, Sport Coupe, Special and Coupe 3P (with its distinctive six rear, circular light units) versions and was followed in 1976 by the new 128, whose appearance and mechanics had been updated to conform with anti-pollution legislation. The 850 reached the end of its lifecycle in 1978 when the Ritmo made its debut. However, prior to this model, which marked a new era in terms of production and communications, including style and the use of plastic materials, mention must be made of the 1971 127 (renewed six years later). It was created to replace the 850 and was given a modern hatchback design (it already had the tailgate

in 1972), which was produced in collaboration with Pio Manzù (son of the famous sculptor Giacomo) and made the car very spacious. After making its debut in 1972, it remained in the range for 16 years, three more than the 126, and was the result of the crisis as it was given the mechanics and DNA of a 500 with modern shapes (it was a small version of the 127) without renouncing solidity and, above-all, operating affordability. Further up in the category was the 1972 132, which drew on the 125. This was the first Fiat assembled by the robots in Mirafiori and the first to leave the production lines with an external rear-view mirror. This detail would be accompanied by others, including those related to safety (such as a steering column that collapsed in five sections to protect the driver), which made it the brand's flagship in 1977 when the 130 left the scene and when it was restyled (side bands and more sophisticated outfitting). The 131 was below the 132. It was 1974 and this car stood out right away because it envisaged two front ends, one with rectangular lights for the basic version and

the Special, with four circular headlights. Four years later it was the turn of the new versions, the Mirafiori and the SuperMirafiori, which were also available in diesel versions, recognizable for the hump on the engine hood, and equipped with rectangular light units, plastic bumpers and side bands. But the 131's calling card was the Abarth Rally, which won three international rally titles, 17 first places in world races and 23 in European races. And then there was the Ritmo, which was new from head to toe, starting with its name, which ended the numeric titles used for previous models. For the first time in the world, bodies were assembled by a robotized system, bumpers remained intact after small blows thanks to polypropylene elastic, internal and external design and components were all rounded and it had novel levers, handles and gauges. In short, this was Fiat's new deal, a vehicle that remained in production until 1988 and became even more exclusive in 1982 with its Super versions, from which the stage was stolen in 1980 by that icon and revolutionary vehicle called the Panda.

222-223 Extremely elegant and charming, the Fiat 130 made its debut in 1969 to replace the brand's flagship, the 2300L. In 1971, a Coupe version of this company car was also produced. It was just as elegant and unique, both in terms of its square shape and its sedan-like body.

223 right In the 70s the Fiat range of vehicles was broad, starting with economy cars up to large sedans. Here are the 1971 127, which replaced the glorious 850, the original and innovative (especially in terms of the materials used) 1978 Ritmo, which took the place of the spacious 128, the 1974 131 Mirafiori taking the place of the 124 and seen here in a special three-door version, and the 1972 132, which replaced the 125 and shown here in its elegant 1974 Gls 1800 version.

Great, small automobiles: The Autobianchi A112 and the Mini Innocenti

Seventeen and ten: this is the number of years for which these small masterpieces were sold, especially their sports versions. Both the Autobianchi 112 and

duction continued of the Primula, the guinea pig on which Fiat experimented front-wheel drive (which was later transferred to the 128), and the tailgate that

gauge, a small steering wheel with three spokes and an engine with an unforgettable sound. The small car was well liked, had personality, was pleasant, had mod-

224 top October 14, 1965, the Duke of Edinburgh traveled to Milan to visit the Innocenti factories. He is seen here on an Innocenti Mini Minor, the version of the famous Mini by Alex Issigonis built in Italy under license from the English manufacturer.

224-225 The complete range of the fifth series of one of Italy's iconic city cars. The Autobianchi A112 was a comfortable, affordable four-seater economy car, seen here in its 1979 version (starting left) with the Junior version (and its cloth roof that could be opened), the Elegant, the Elite and the sporty Abarth. Two other generations of this vehicle would follow, ending the production cycle in 1986 after 17 honorable years and 1.3 million units manufactured.

225 top Italian singer Wilma De Angelis about to get in a new Austin A40. Fighter Duilio Loi is behind the wheel. It is October 21, 1960 in the Innocenti factories in Milan and this new vehicle is about to be presented. It was manufactured by Ferdinando Innocenti under BMC license.

electronic ignition. Much is known about the Mini and its original 1959 version, designed by Alec Issigonis. On the other hand, little is known about Ferdinando

who in turn was able to convince his father to manufacture foreign automobiles under license in Italy. After a first attempt with the A40 by BMC Austin, his

from 1965 to 1975. In the meantime, Innocenti changed ownership to first become Iri, followed by Leyland in 1971 for the portion concerning automo-

Not just on the track: from Formula One to rallies

Formula One changed hands. The main protagonists of the rainbow-colored circus in the sixties were the English and garage owners, however Italians still had Ferrari waving the Italian flag with pride. It won the 1961 world championship through Phil Hill in addition to the manufacturer's title, and similarly in 1964 with John Surtees in the driver's seat and then with Niki Lauda in 1975 and 1977. The manufacturer's title was won by Ferrari in 1976 too and Jody Sheckter also had a double victory in 1979. But this 20-year period focused attention on another discipline: rallies. The cars used were taken from production models, whose sales were positively influenced by their successes in races on wildly varying surfaces, from snow to mud and desert sand, on five continents, all of which forced manufacturers to be more technically prepared. This explained the international domination by Lancia, first with its Fulvia Coupe and later with the Stratos, which brought drivers like Sandro Munari to the fore. Fiat entered the scene in the 1970s with the Fiat 124 and 131 plus the Autobianchi A112, all very strong and able to dominate in Italy and Europe. Alfa Romeo didn't just sit back and watch from the side lines. GT and prototype races became its business, first with the Giulietta, followed by the uncatchable Giulia TZ and the unforgettable 33. The Milanese manufacturer officially returned to racing, having pulled out in 1951 after winning two Formula One championships. Formula One was in its blood and the *Biscione* made its comeback in 1979 as the engine supplier for Brabham and later with its own single-seater.

226 Phil Hill, close to his cup and wearing the laurel wreath, celebrates his victorious Formula One Italy Grand Prix in Monza in 1961. It took him two hours, three minutes and 13 seconds to travel the 267 miles (430 km) in his Ferrari. He was one of only 12 out of the original 32 drivers to cross the finish line.

226-227 Niki Lauda on a Ferrari at the 1974 English Grand Prix on the Brands Hatch Circuit. He came in fifth after having obtained pole position and raced the fastest lap.

227 bottom A race in the rain for the unforgettable Austrian driver Niki Lauda, seen here on Ferrari 312 T2 no. 11 at the 1977 Austrian Grand Prix on the Osterreichring Circuit at the chicane. He finished second in this race.

228 top Young Alain Delon in a racing suit poses near the futuristic Lancia Stratos. Even the French actor could not resist his fascination for automobile races – especially rallies – and the thrills provided by the Italian trademark's winning vehicle.

228 bottom The Stratos was an original vehicle with a futuristic wedge shape, and was the queen of rallies from 1973 until 1982. It was the work of Bertone and was produced on a Fulvia 1.6HF chassis equipped with the Dino Ferrari V6 2.4L (2418 cc), 192 hp engine. Five hundred units were manufactured to obtain type-approval for racing.

228-229 The 1968 Lancia Fulvia 1.6 HF was intended for racing and led the Turinese manufacturer towards important rally victories, including the one obtained by the Munari-Mannuccia Team at the 1972 Monte Carlo Rally, which led to the creation of the Montecarlo 1.35 version.

CHAPTER 6

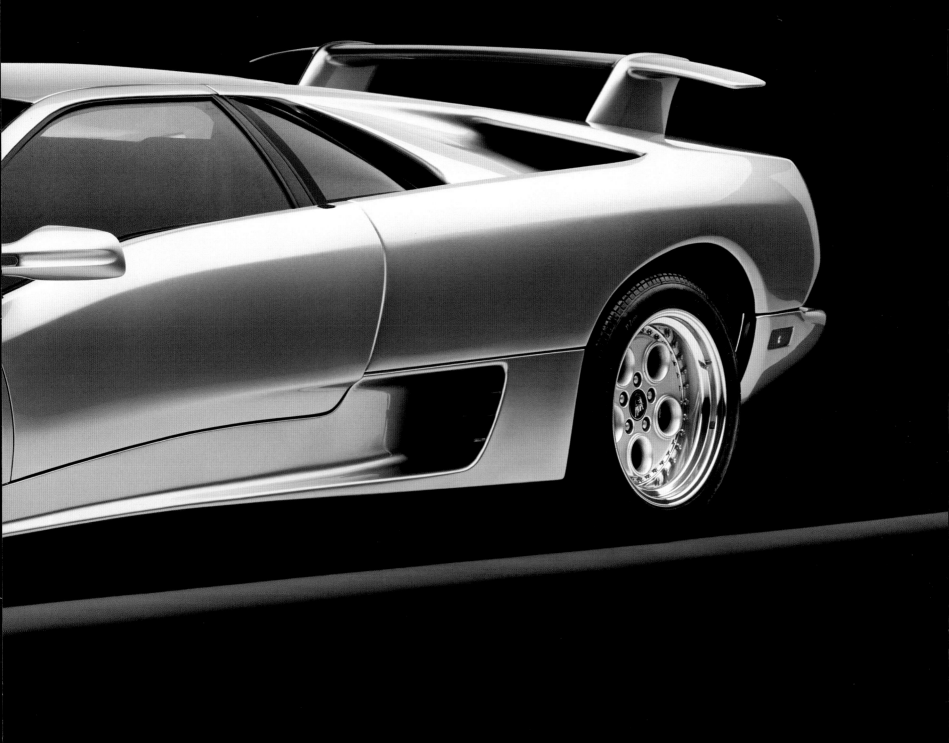

Towards the new millennium amidst open markets, strong foreign competition and with no alliances

I n the 1980s, as the new millennium approached, amidst open markets, strong foreign competition and with no alliances, the Italian automobile scene started to take its current appearance. At least in terms of market composition, which included the arrival of Asian car manufacturers and an increasing number of European models (German and French primarily), so much so that by 1997, imported cars exceeded those manufactured domestically. During the final 20 years of the century, foreign car manufacturers developed alliances and made agreements with other international manufacturers to be more competitive in all segments of the market. This was a market that was taking large steps towards becoming global, and the European market was opening its doors to Eastern Europe after the drawing back of the Iron Curtain. And so, while Volkswagen, together with Audi, took over Seat in Spain, Skoda in the Czech Republic, Bugatti in France, Bentley in Great Britain and Lamborghini in Italy, Ford went shopping in Japan (Mazda) and in Europe and

bought Land Rover and Jaguar from across the English Channel, along with Volvo in Sweden. General Motors purchased Saab in Sweden and Daewoo in Korea, Renault took over Romania's Dacia and then BMW conquered Rover (which it later sold) and Mini. Italy was left standing because the policy of the Fiat Group – the only automobile company in the country able to compete with these foreign behemoths – was to pursue differentiation. Cars were no longer its core business and therefore it did not consider the offer made by Ford or the acquisition of Chrysler and Volvo. This *preference* led to a series of weak products that were unsuccessful in segments such as the mid-size car (Bravo-Brava, Stilo for Fiat, 145-146 for Alfa Romeo, Dedra and Lybra for Lancia), where the Group had traditionally been very competitive. The result was that motorists turned to foreign products. Some niches endured, such as the minivans, a phenomenon of the 1990s inherited from the United States. This followed the Fiat-PSA (Peugeot-Citröen) agreement for the joint production of a model that was the same for everyone, with a few different aesthetic changes, such

as the front end. It was called Ulysse for Fiat, Zeta for Lancia, 807 for Peugeot and Evasion for Citröen. The Italian-French agreement also led to another interesting product with regard to commercial vehicles, and brought to light the Fiat Ducato and its siblings, the Peugeot Boxer and Citröen Jumper.

It was said that mid-size cars were the backbone (in excess of 30 percent) of the car fleet circulating in Italy, a country whose market was growing, especially thanks to developments in Southern Italy. In 1988 more than two million units were delivered there (2,131,197, source: UNRAE), making it the most densely populated area in the new century. Mention should also be made of the changes to the fleet of circulating vehicles over this 20-year period, which attested to the social wellbeing of and growth in the population. In the eighties, small cars (up to 0.8L, 800 cc) had 24.7 percent of the market share, but this number decreased in the nineties to 16.5 percent. On the contrary, mid-large size cars (1.5L-2.0L, 1500-2000 cc) increased from 9.6 percent to 19.4 percent and large cars (exceeding 2.0L, 2000 cc) more than dou-

bled in popularity, from 1.7 percent to 3.8 percent. This latter phenomenon was also thanks to the abolition of the 38 percent VAT (value added tax) on the purchase price of new vehicles with engines exceeding 2.0L (2000 cc) and 2.5L (2500 cc) if it was a diesel. Diesel was a prominent representative for the period, which changed the tastes of motorists and to which great technical attention was paid, making it more than competitive with gas engines in terms of performance as it offered the added value of significantly better consumption by using noble-mixture-driven engines. Diesel units made huge strides forward and increased boost pressure thanks to turbo, intercooler, variable geometric turbines, four-valve cylinder heads, direct injection, injection-pump and the revolutionary common rail created by Fiat with Magneti-Marelli (and then sold to Bosch). The return on sales was predictable and the new millennium benefitted from the results of these investments in diesel models, so much so that in 2004 the percentage of registered diesel vehicles outnumbered gas-operated vehicles. This was the return match for this

engine, which had always been considered poor, smoky, slow and the prerogative of trucks, and had been oppressed since 1976 by the so-called super road tax that limited its distribution. It was only able to take off in 1992 when heavy taxation paved the way for triennial exemptions based on pollution categories, which were extended in 1998, and until the taxation was finally abolished in 2005.

Diesel engines were not the only vehicles to ride the wave of progress and innovation. Environmental concerns forced manufacturers to show their green thumbs and to introduce technological improvements such as electronic injection in place of carburetors in fuel systems, catalytic mufflers for exhaust devices with lead gas that had very little time left and variable valve timing engines. Then streamlined manufacturing systems arrived from Japan to improve efficiency and reduce costs. The same logic resulted in communities for which platforms and engines were developed and used as a base to be assembled on several vehicles, not only within the same range but also for the different brands in the group.

230-231 The 1993 four-wheel drive Lamborghini Diablo (seen here in its Vt Viscous traction version) was an extreme icon of the sports car and wild car of the 1990s. It survived various changes in corporate ownership unscathed and remained in production from 1990 to 2001. Its doors opened upwards and it was equipped with powerful mechanics and a V12, 590 hp engine that could reach a maximum speed of mph (325 km/h).

232 left The Lancia Lybra was manufactured from 1999 to 2006 in sedan and station wagon versions. Its large front headlamps carry the brand's distinctive look. It was equipped with one of three gas-operated (1.6L, 1.8L and 2.0L, – 1600 1800 or 2000 cc) with four valves per cylinder) or two diesel-operated (1.9L and 2.4L – 1900 and 2400 cc) engines.

232 right and 233 left These vehicles, the Fiat Bravo and Brava, debuted in 1995 to replace the Tipo, standing out due to their hatchback or fastback-sedan bodies. They were both very spacious and the Bravo was quite successful with the public, especially the younger crowd. Various engines included the turbo-diesel, intercooler and new Common Rail direct injection system, which revolutionized the world of diesel vehicles by improving performance and reducing consumption and emissions.

233 right The Fiat Ulysse was the result of the joint venture with the PSA Group (Peugeot-Citroën). This minivan made its debut in 1994 and was distinguished by its spacious driver and passenger compartment, which could seat up to eight people in three rows.

Ferrari after the Drake

Enzo Ferrari died in August of 1988 but his car manufacturing company did not suffer as a result. The transfer of 90 percent of the company to Fiat and the appointment in 1991 of Luca Cordero di Montezemolo as chairman started a process of metamorphosis resulting in great success in future years, especially in the field of racing. In the meantime, road-legal production experienced a golden era thanks to the debuts of a series of models-icons, which brought about many innovations and revolutions, and bore witness to the great and precious technical heritage accumulated by Maranello during its racing experience. It all started with the 288 GTO and the Testarossa. The former stood out for its powerful performance – 190 mph (305 km/h) and 0-62 mph (0-100 km/h) in five seconds –, not only obtained with a V8 double-turbocharged, 2.9L (2,855 cc), 400 hp engine, but also thanks to the use of innovative materials such as com-

posites mutated by aerospace engineering used to shape the chassis, or the super light but solid Kevlar on the hood and tail end. Starting in 1992, the Testarossa became the 512TR and then, two years later, the F512M (Modificata). It should be remembered for its design with a strong tail end and side grills that not only influenced and hid but provided air to an innovative cooling system composed of two radiators assembled on the side of the central engine. It was created based

on the 512BBi, contained mechanical gems such as four-valve per cylinder head and electronic injection and ignition and it aimed at international success by relying heavily on its combination of elegance and performance, as dictated by *Made in Italy*. The turn of the 328 (GTB, GTS, and also Turbo) came in 1985. This replaced the basic 308 model in the range and was more powerful (270 hp) and even more attractive (designed by Pininfarina).

254-255 *The Ferrari Testarossa made its debut in 1984 to replace the 512 BB (from which it got the basics). It was created to strict American standards so that it could be exported overseas. This was a supercar, intended to become the pride of Made in Italy around the world, thanks also to its name, which was well-known among enthusiasts. Electronics, two cooling radiators located on the side (explaining the large, side air intakes) and exceptional performance were the stand-out features of this Ferrari, and its various iterations (512 TR and 512 Modificata) remained in production for 12 years until 1996. A respectable total of 8428 units were produced.*

But the spotlights all shone on the F40 and F50, which made their debuts in 1987 and 1997, on the occasion of the brand's 40th and 50th anniversaries, respectively. They were technological laboratories on four wheels and offered the best know-how gained in Formula One and transferred to road-legal production.

Lightness was the key word and it is curious to see how this was developed by the two dream cars during the 10-year interval by highlighting the technological progress made in the meantime. The F40 flaunted a composite structure: carbon fiber was combined with Kevlar, which resulted in a system that allowed integrated engine control and strong and super-sporty profiles (they all had large rear spoilers and an infinite number of air intakes). These developments were the result of the new wind tunnel, first used in 1986, and completed the cycle of corporate development after the expansion in the previous decade of the factory, paint shop and track at Fiorano. The F50 was essentially less of a racing car, although not when it came to performance. The track or the road made no difference to this car, and it could have been a Barchetta or coupe, thanks to its hard top. The result of wind and aerodynamics, Pininfarina gave it an enviable silhouette, while its strong profiles and mechanics were molded on a carbon monocoque shell. Innovations included cast iron brakes obtained with a hub made by Brembo, special tires that could be used both on the track and road

236-237 The 1987 Ferrari F40 was the vehicle made to celebrate the company's first 40 years. It was inspired by the 288 Gto and was practically a dream car that could be used both on the road and track. It was made with materials such as carbon and Kevlar and implemented high-tech solutions often taken from Formula One. Its V8 3.0L (2936 cc) engine with two turbochargers provided 478 hp and reached a maximum speed of 201 mph (324 km/h).

238-239 The Ferrari 360 Modena made its debut in 1999 and represented the new style of the prancing stallion's coupes and sports cars for the new millennium – basically those basic models in the range representing two-thirds of total production. The Modena included the use of aluminum as a structural material and it was equipped with a V8 4.0L (3586 cc), 445 hp engine located centrally or in the back. It remained in production for five years, along with the 360 Spider, which was presented in 2000.

and a rubber tank. Its V12, 4.7L (4.700 cc), 520 hp engine reached 202 mph (325 km/h) and acted as the supporting structure for the transmission-suspensions-differential unit. The result was that 349 units, produced over two years, were sold before they were even produced, for two million dollars each. There were other cult vehicles in addition to these two. The 1989 Mondial T, also convertible, replaced the Mondial 8 and was presented as a true four-seater with a longitudinal engine and transversal transmission (hence the "T"). This solution had been used in Formula One in the 1970s and allowed Niki Lauda and Jody Scheckter to win titles in 1975, 1977 and 1979. The saga of the T model also continued with the 348 coupe and open sports car, whose style was taken from the Testarossa. They were first replaced in 1995 by the F355GT and GTS with a new V8, 3.5L (3500 cc), 380 hp engine and later in 1999 by the 360 Modena, which became available in a Spider version the following year. The idea of a comfortable four-seater returned in the 1992 456 GT (it became Modificata in 1998). Elegance and sophistication best described this grand touring car. It was very fast but comfortable for long trips, re-introduced a front engine and was also equipped in 1996 with an automatic transmission that was highly regarded in the US and Japan. The millennium ended with the 1996 550 Maranello coupe, which would continue in the new century through the Barchetta Pininfarina and 575M Maranello versions.

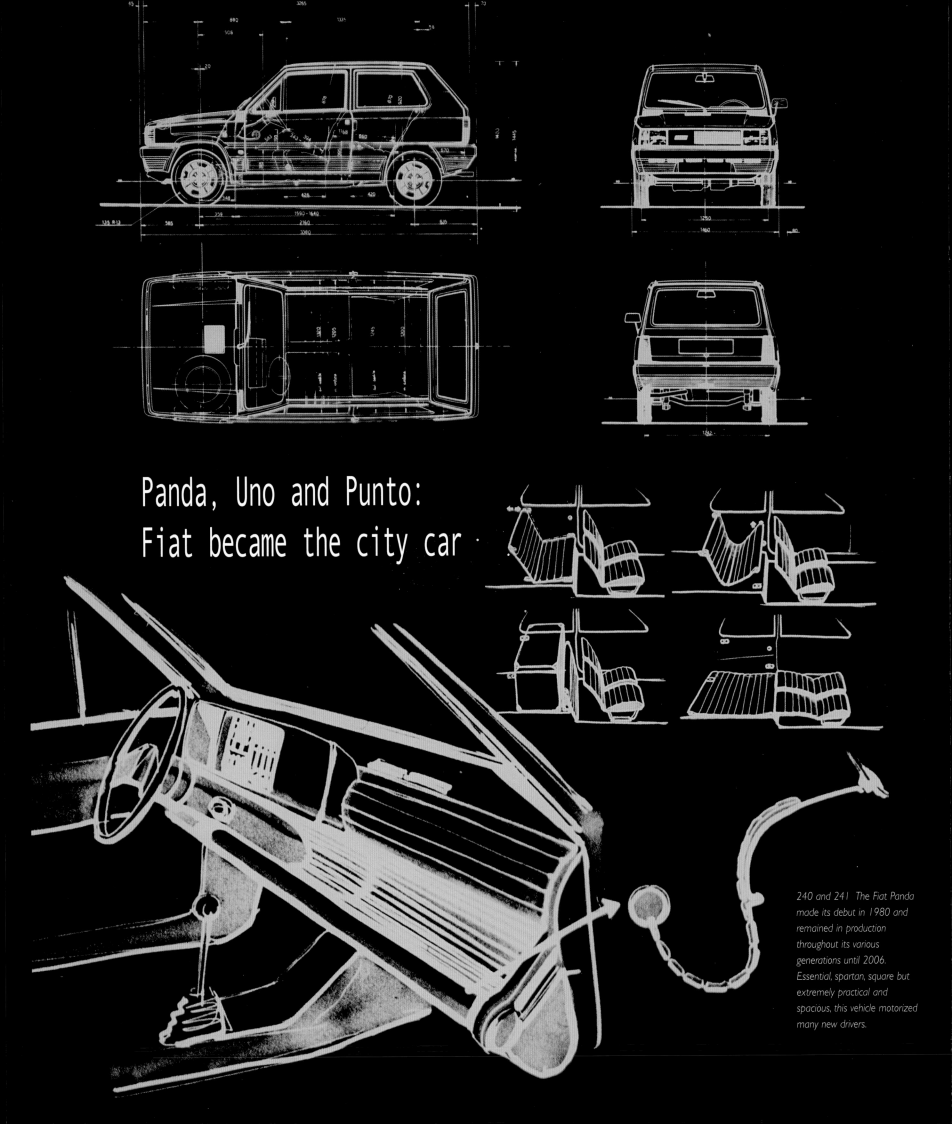

Panda, Uno and Punto:
Fiat became the city car

240 and 241 The Fiat Panda made its debut in 1980 and remained in production throughout its various generations until 2006. Essential, spartan, square but extremely practical and spacious, this vehicle motorized many new drivers.

Under the management of Cesare Romiti (who had become president in 1980), Fiat inherited very successful models such as the Panda and Uno, the first of which was designed by Giugiaro. The Panda represented significant new developments for the Group as it marked the return of the front engine (the 500 and the 126 had rear engines) and was the first time a project had been assigned externally. It was square, basic, practical and equipped with solutions such as generous external buffering bands to protect it from the minor bumps and marks that are inevitably collected when parking in the city, an interior fitted with a large pocket running the entire length of the dashboard, a mobile ashtray, seats that looked like deckchairs and allowed all movement and exceptional loads for a vehicle only 11 ft (3.38 m) long, as well as a driver and passenger compartment with enough room for five people, thanks to its expanded height. Its simple, indestructible mechanics housed two engines, a twin-cylinder air-cooled 0.7L (652 cc), 30 hp engine and a second 0.9L (903 cc), 45 hp engine. The Panda was a marvelous car for recently qualified drivers, highly requested by women and by those who lived in the mountains (the 4x4 couldn't be stopped and was the preferred vehicle of the Italian forest-ranger corps and those who provided services at high elevations). It was such a success that it stayed in production in various versions (such as the Super, 4x4, Selecta with an automatic transmission CVT, 1100 IE with electronic fuel injection) for 23 years and has always been near the top of the list of Italy's best-selling cars.

The Uno made its debut in 1983 and was launched at Cape Canaveral, demonstrating its intent to be successful both in Italy and abroad. It was a little more spacious than the Panda, but had more rounded profiles, a more modern design and a more sophisticated interior. Giorgio Forattini's advertising campaign was pleasant and practical and claimed that "The Uno is comfortable, affordable, chic, and feisty." It proposed innovative solutions such as the single-blade windshield wiper, and its unique dashboard with two satellites on the side of the steering wheel for primary and secondary controls. The Uno's 15-year career was actually longer because, although production in Italy ceased in 1995, it continued in other markets such as Brazil and Morocco, where it was still very successful. It had several engine types during this time: gas, diesel, turbo gas and diesel, even an energy-saving version that was particularly geared towards reducing consumption, with a cut-off system that interrupted the flow of gas during the release phase or the presence of an on-board econometer indicating instant consumption and when to change gears. In 1984, it was the turn of the Regata, which replaced the 131 and was proposed as a mid-size sedan with an additional station wagon, called the Weekend, distinguishable by its rear tailgate and a tailboard that favored loading. The next was the Croma, a replacement for the unlucky Argenta and the result of the Tipo 4 project, which also led to the creation of the Alfa Romeo 164, Lancia Thema and Saab 9000 with the same loading platform. Comfortable and super fast thanks to powerful turbo gas and diesel engines and a direct-injection version, it was characterized by a fastback sedan profile with a practical and versatile tailgate. Production savings for the Tipo 4 project led to the Tipo 2, which for Fiat and Alfa Romeo meant a platform able to house models with 23 different gas and diesel engines and common mechanical and outfit-

242 top One of Fiat's masterpieces was the Fiat Uno. Over 6.5 million units were sold in its 12-year career.

242 bottom The 1993 Fiat Punto took after the Uno and retained Fiat's supremacy among city cars for 13 years (six million units were sold).

ting elements. The 1988 Tipo was the first outcome of this project. Called upon to replace the Ritmo, it was a hatchback with a front end that would be common to many future models. It had room for five passengers and several outfitting gems such as digital instrumentation, which put the old pointer-type indicators to rest.

Other results of the Tipo 2 were the Tempra (replacing the Regata), which was in turn replaced by the Marea, the Bravo and the Brava after the Tipo, and the Coupe. The latter marked the return of Fiat to the sports car segment after 15 years, since the X1/9, and was presented with a unique

Pininfarina profile and powerful engines (for example, the Turbo 20V achieved 155 mph, 250 km/h). The Barchetta was also a thrilling model and an agile and pleasant open sports car, while the Ulysse marked the entrance onto the market of minivans through this functional model (even an eight-seater) equipped with sliding rear side doors and providing the comfort of a large sedan. The 1993 Punto led to good results for Fiat after the automobile crisis at the beginning of the 1990s. It replaced the Uno and didn't fear the increasing international competition, which included the Ford Fiesta, the Opel Corsa, the Renault Clio, the Nissan Micra, the Peugeot 206 and

the Volkswagen Polo, among others, thanks to its pleasant design, a welcoming driver and passenger compartment, reliable mechanics and an enriched selection of engines in addition to the convertible, the last body work done by *Nuccio* Bertone, who died in 1997.

The 20-year period ended with the small Seicento and the Multipla, another six-seater minivan (two rows) that was more compact than the Ulysse (13 ft – 4.09 m – long) but very capable and had a unique design that wasn't always well accepted. It was also available in methane or LPG versions and was popular among taxi drivers.

242-243 The Fiat Barchetta sports car made its debut in 1995 and was highly regarded for its simple lines that were reminiscent of the convertibles from the 1950s. It was very affordable, to the delight of young people, who could drive this convertible without sustaining excessive maintenance costs, thanks also to a gas-operated 1.8L (1800 cc) engine that provided performance without excessive consumption.

Lancia Thema and Alfa Romeo 164, great Italian flagships

Lancia and Alfa Romeo experienced many common situations in this period under the aegis of Fiat with the Tipo 2 and Tipo 4 projects, which led to a series of models, some of which became true icons for the period. Certainly the flagships, Thema and the 164, were in first place. They were two large sedans by Lancia and Alfa, half of the four-of-a-kind that also included the Fiat Croma and the Saab 9000. The 1984

244-245 The Lancia Thema 2, released in 1988, continued the tradition of the Italian flagship, which shone together with the Alfa Romeo 164 and the Fiat Croma and shared the same platform and engines. This new generation of the Thema stood out for its modified front end. It remained in production until 1994.

245 top The Lancia Beta was also produced in a sedan version and made its debut in 1980 with the Trevi, which stayed in production for four years. The Volumex version was added in 1982 and was equipped with a supercharged engine with a positive displacement compressor that could push this sedan up to 118 mph (190 km/h).

Thema was an immediate success that gratified Lancia enthusiasts and also attracted new clients to make a status symbol of this elegant sedan with sophisticated outfitting (wood finishing and equipped with elements such as an advanced air-conditioner). It also featured a powerful engine, inspired by the IE Turbo with an intercooler and electronic ignition, 160 hp, 135 mph (218 km/h) or the diesel version Turbo ds 2.5 with an

intercooler and 100 hp for those who travelled great distances throughout the year. The Thema was also the first Italian car equipped with ABS, a system to prevent wheels from locking when braking, which improved vehicle control and safety. After the 1987 station wagon came the restyled 1989 Thema 2, after the Thema 8.32 had caused a sensation two years earlier. Better known as the Thema Ferrari because of its sim-

THEMA turbo 16v LX

ilarity to the Stratos, the Thema 8.32 was equipped with a Ferrari 8-cylinder, 32 valve, 3.0L (3000 cc), 215 hp engine like the one used in Maranello for the 328 and Mondial. The features that gave the Thema even greater fame included adjustable electric leather seats designed by Poltrona Frau and a spoiler on the trunk hood that appeared when a specific control was activated by the driver. By 1994 the Thema had reached its third series and it was time for replacements. The K made its debut together with the 1997 coupe, but was not as successful as their predecessor due to an unoriginal profile and somewhat questionable reliability. It was unfortunate because it was equipped with a five-cylinder, 20-valve engine and a very sophisticated

interior. The Delta continued to provide satisfaction and win rally championships all over the world. It became an object of desire in its road-legal versions, the HF Turbo, HF 4wd (four-wheel drive), HF Integrale and Integrale Evoluzione. The Evoluzione was better known as the Deltona and led to many special versions, including two convertibles specially produced for the Agnelli family), which accompanied the successful Delta until 1995. The standard version continued with a second series starting in 1993 and was retired at the beginning of the new millennium. However, the Lancia range included many other models in between the Thema and Delta. One of these was the Prisma, a mid-size sedan that drew from the Thema

and remained in production from 1982 to 1989, including a four-wheel drive version. It was replaced by the Dedra, which was produced until the end of the century, including a popular station wagon version, and was in turn replaced by the Lybra, with its circular lights, an homage to classic cars of the past. The Y was also a magnificent successor to the 1985 Autobianchi Y10, which in turn succeeded the A112 and was extremely successful during its 10-year career, thanks to its original shape (a truncated tail end with a black tailgate). The new Lancia city car was popular for its compact and modern profile and sophisticated outfitting. Its 1.2L (1200 cc) engine was untiring, provided good performance and had contained consumption.

245 bottom The Delta Hf4wd made its debut in 1986 and stood out for its permanent four-wheel drive. It introduced the Delta Hf Integrale, and Integrale 16V versions, as well as the Integrale Evoluzione, also known as the Deltona.

As for the Alfa Romeo, the spotlight was on the 164, which, like the Thema, immediately conquered the public. Its elegant profile (designed by Pininfarina), level outfitting, five-star performance, front-wheel drive and four-wheel drive Q4 version were combined with a V6, 3.0L (3000 cc), 231 hp engine with six gears able to reach a maximum speed of 143 mph (230 km/h). The 164 also took off in the United States and the Far East, where it was called the 168 (four is considered a negative number in China). After a 10-year career, it made room for the 166, while the 33 stayed in production for one more year (it had replaced the Alfasud in 1983). It was equipped with boxer engines and was very successful, thanks especially to the Giardinetta and insertable 4x4 versions, and the exclusive Quadrifoglio Oro version. The 1985 75, celebrating the brand's 75th anniversary, was also regarded positively. It is remembered for its very high back end, double-ignition Twin Spark engines that improved performance, a 90 hp diesel engine that made it the fastest turbo diesel in the world when it was launched, and the Milan versions with large bumpers destined for the United States. At Alfa, it was also time for sports cars; 1989 was the year of a 100 million Lira model that would become an object of desire, the SZ, and it also came in a convertible version, the RZ. These two vehicles were *outfitted* by Zagato and were produced in just 19 months by a team with a design center headed by Walter de Silva (already the creator of such enthusiastic concepts as the Proteo and the Nuvola), Giorgio Pianta from Alfa corse, Elio and Gianni Zagato, and Giuseppe Bizzarrini (son of the great car designer, Giotto). These dream cars had a huge impact, implemented carbon (also for the dashboard), had a very sporty wedge-shaped profile and a front end with six rectangular lights. They immediately captured the hearts of Alfa enthusiasts despite their front-wheel drive, and the 1000 units produced, plus 350 Roadster versions, were sold immediately.

The 1993 155 also revived many sporty memories. It replaced the 75 and was built on the same platform as the Fiat Tempra and Lancia Dedra. Used in touring car races with GTA and V6 TI versions, the road-legal versions were equipped with Twin Spark engines, technology used again in 1994 on the 145 and 146. The 145 was very successful with its very high, almost truncated tail end, while the 146 was a fastback sedan. The 1994 Spider and GTV were Alfa Romeo's sports cars, and their names were throwbacks to the glorious past. The shape of the coupe and convertible was certainly original and best interpreted the concept of the wedge-shaped profile so loved by Alfa enthusiasts, while there was also a return to the past with the handle used on the 1997 156, which drew from the design of the 1900 model and re-launched the brand's sales and image. A very successful vehicle in terms of appearance, mechanics and engine size, the 156 was the first to flaunt the innovative diesel common rail engines. These were like a Copernican revolution in diesel units, thanks to an unheard of high-pressure injection system that improved performance and reduced consumption and emissions. In the year 2000 came the turn of the Sportwagon, Alfa's version of a station wagon, which was feisty but offered a rather unexceptional load capacity.

246 and 247 This vehicle marked Alfa Romeo's new journey and brought success back to the Milanese manufacturer. It is the 156, which was presented in 1997 and had many of the brand's stylistic elements, such as the large front screen, rounded hood and aggressive lines. It was also equipped with engines that matched its sportiness, including diesel-operated 16-valve units with Common Rail injection (above) and twin spark ignition gas-operated engines. The Gta version (below) shone bright at Touring races.

Alejandro De Tomaso's brand wanted to create a large but affordable vehicle with a displacement that did not exceed 2.0L (2000 cc), so as to avoid onerous taxation, while still in keeping with the manufacturer's heritage, which meant high performance and quality outfitting. The result was the Biturbo. Compact (13 ft – 4.15 m – long) and aggressive, this coupe attracted attention at the 1981 Turin Auto Show, thanks to the sophisticated outfitting of the driver and passenger compartment, which incorporated large quantities of leather and wood and included an analogue, oval-shaped clock that dominated the center of the dashboard, and instrumentation on a blue background. It flaunted a V6, 2.0L (1.996 cc), 180 hp engine with two Citröen-Maserati turbochargers. Its price, 22 million Lira, made it an affordable dream for many and absolutely competitive with respect to the strong German competition. In addition, the fact it was manufactured in Milan at the Innocenti plants in Lambrate was another reason for Italians to purchase it. Unfortunately, reliability problems undermined its success and its sales, despite an expanding range over the years that included four-door versions (420 and 425), the Spyder, the new 430, 222 and 422, the Karif two-seater coupe and the Shamal, Racing and Ghibli in 1990-1992. These models were already part of the new course taken by Maserati, which sold 49 percent of its equity to the Fiat Group in 1989; De Tomas had originally sold this share to Lee Iacocca's Chrysler in the hopes of eventually selling the entire company. Fiat still owned 100 percent of the equity in 1993, but

The object of desire: the Maserati Biturbo

later sold 50 percent in 1997 and then the remainder in 1999 to Ferrari to create an all-Italian sports dream car company. This period included models such as the 1992 Barchetta, created for racing, the 1994 Quattroporte Evoluzione, with its concept of a super flagship with softened shapes, and the 1998 3200 GT, designed by Giugiaro and the first progeny of the transfer to the *Prancing Stallion*. This fascinating vehicle is still requested by collectors today and is unforgettable for its highly sought-after rear LED light units.

248-249 The Maserati Biturbo (seen here in its 1985 Spider version) was manufactured in Milan at the Innocenti plants. It combined prestigious materials and finishing touches with an engine with two turbochargers (hence 'Biturbo').

249 top The Maserati Shamal was presented in December 1989, at the same time as Fiat's 49% acquisition of the company. It had the same chassis as the Biturbo and a very sporty body. It was equipped with a V8 3.2L (3217 cc), 326 hp engine that was able to reach 168 mph (270 km/h).

250 and 251   The Maserati 3200 Gt was presented in 1998 and was a model created under Ferrari management. Designed by Giugiaro, this was a marvelous coupe with a unique tail end and LED lamps, which were revolutionary for the period and a precursor to the current trend. This coupe's elegant and sophisticated interior continued the tradition of the Tridente and was equipped with a V8 3.2L (3217 cc) engine with double turbochargers. This version was fine-tuned by Ferrari technicians and provided 368 hp, allowing the vehicle to reach 174 mph (280 km/h). Its Brembo brake system was a modified Formula-One version.

Stories of Italian dream cars: Lamborghini, Isotta Fraschini, Bugatti and Pagani

252 top The powerful tail end of a Lamborghini Diablo Vt. Four hundred units were manufactured, giving life to the Roadster, Sv (sport veloce) and to the Vtt with a supercharged engine with four turbines.

252-253 This Lamborghini Jalpa dates back to 1981 and stayed in production for seven years. It was equipped with an eight-cylinder engine and was the last Lambo made by Lamborghini. Its unique removable metal top made it a true "targa". A total of 421 units were produced. As it is a hard, pure, high-strung sports car designed for those who know how to drive (no efforts were made to make it comfortable), it is quite highly sought after by collectors.

In 1980, once out of bankruptcy and owned by French entrepreneur Patrick Mimran, the new Lamborghini put former Maserati member Giulio Alfieri in charge of technical management and also appointed him president to re-launch the brand. During this decade it presented models such as the new Countach 5000 Quattrovalvole and Anniversario, the Jalpa, derived from the Urraco, and later the Diablo, which was the sole protagonist of the nineties and the last model to leave Sant'Agata Bolognese. This dream car was able to singly sustain the fate of the brand sold to Chrysler in 1987, which in turn sold 60 percent to Tommy Suharto (son of the former Indonesian president) in 1993, the year in which founder Ferruccio Lamborghini died, and the remaining 40 percent to Malaysian company Malaysiàs Mycom, to then end up in the Volkswagen Group at Audi in 1998. The Diablo's mechanics were exaggerated (V12, 5.7L – 5707 cc – and 492 hp engine), it performed astonishingly

(202 mph – 325 km/h –, acceleration from 0-62 mph – 0-100 km/h – in four seconds) and its upward-opening doors gave it a striking appearance. In short, it had all the elements of a super car with track performance and was favored by the public, considering the 2900 units sold in various versions, including the Roadster. This was a public that, for a moment, thought it could dream of purchasing an Isotta Fraschini, a highly-regarded brand, especially abroad. Coachbuilder Fissore in Cherasco bought out the trademark from Finmeccanca and used state contributions to build a factory in the province of Reggio Calabria to assemble a high-performing model whose mechanical heritage and chassis were taken from Audi. The T8 and T12 were created in 1998, but the German car manufacturer ended relations with Lamborghini in the meantime and ceased collaboration with Fissore, which stopped the project, put the enterprise into bankruptcy and dissolved hopes of a re-

turn of the legendary Isotta Fraschini. Another illusion was the return of Bugatti, which made its comeback in 1987 with Romano Artioli, Suzuki's importer for Italy and Bugatti International (it used the trademark for other productions), and with technical sponsors who built a factory in Campogalliano in the province of Modena. The factory was equipped with an engine test bench to test the new V12, 3.5L (3500 cc), 560 hp engine equipping the carbon EB110 (acronym for Ettore Bugatti's 110th birthday), which made its debut in Paris in 1991. The first of the 126 units were delivered the following year and included a standard version, S 600 hp and SS version (a yellow one was purchased by Michael Schumacher). There was also room for the beautiful 1993 sports EB112, designed by Giugiaro and the precursor to the current four-door coupe. But the new Bugatti models were not as successful as had been hoped and Artioli & Co. was forced to declare bankruptcy in 1995.

254-255 *The Lamborghini Raptor Zagato made its debut as a show car at the 1996 Geneva Auto Show. It weighed 661 lbs (300 kg) less than a Diablo Vt and was equipped with a V12 5.7L (5700 cc) engine positioned in the center. With the compressor, the engine's power could reach 629 hp and a maximum speed of 205 mph (330 km/h).*

256-257 *A look at the central, tail end of this Lamborghini Raptor Zagato, with large air intakes to cool its V12 engine. This dream car was auctioned off by Brooks at the 2000 Geneva Auto Show to a private American collector for US$236,000.*

258-259 This Bugatti Eb 110 from 1991 belonged to the trademark taken over by Roman Artioli in 1987. Its carbon chassis was created by the French aerospace industry, its V12 3.5L (3499 cc) aluminum engine was equipped with four turbochargers and it had five valves for each cylinder and four-wheel drive. The car's 50 hp allowed it to reach a maximum speed of 218 mph (351 km/h). Production of the vehicle ceased in 1995 when the company went bankrupt, at which time the vehicle was on the market for US$370,000. One of the Ss versions (a variation of the Eb110) was purchased by Michael Schumacher.

However, Pagani remained an active manufacturer of very fast four-wheel dreams. This company was established in Modena by Argentinean Horacio Pagani, a former Lamborghini employee and friend of Juan Manuel Fangio. He was highly talented and had an ardent passion for automobiles. First he restyled the Lamborghini Countach Anniversario and then realized his dream of manufacturing his own car with his own trademark, which he tested in the Dallara wind tunnel and equipped with a Mercedes V12 engine. The result was the Zonda C12 (named after a wind in the Andes) coupe or roadster, 555 hp and capable of reaching 211 mph (340 km/h). These models are still being produced in their natural evolutions and at times their price far exceeds 1 million euros.

Formula One, rallies, touring car races and prototype racing: there was something for everyone

Power exceeding 1000 hp, an obsession for aerodynamics, the arrival of electronics and new materials like Kevlar and carbon, but also the search for as much driver safety as possible. Formula One evolved but Italy was always among the protagonists, even if Ferrari didn't do very well until it won the manufacturer's title in 1999, with a driver in Michael Schumacher who was closing in on unforgettable successes. It had won the manufacturer's ti-

tle in 1982 and 1983, Michele Alboreto came close to the driver's title in 1985 and Ayrton Senna thrilled the public in the red cars. His career came to a tragic end in 1994 during the San Marino Grand Prix. Alfa Romeo also participated in the Formula One, but it left it in 1985 and sold out to Osella the same year that Minardi was founded, resulting in the debut of drivers such as Nannini, Trulli, Fisichella and Alonso.

262 top The Ferrari pits at the Formula One Italian Grand Prix Monza Circuit in 1985. Gianni Agnelli stopped briefly to speak with Italian driver Michele Alboreto behind the wheel of a single seater Ferrari. That year the Italian driver would be the Formula One World Championship runner-up.

262 bottom A frowning Luca Cordero di Montezemolo in the Ferrari area at the Japanese Grand Prix in Suzuka in November 1998. Mika Hakkinen on a McLaren-Mercedes won the race and the drivers' championship after Michael Schumacher had tire problems.

262-263 Ferrari C126 C3 no. 28 of French Ferrari driver René Arnoux races towards victory at the German Grand Prix on the Hockenheim Circuit in 1983.

Italian gratification had to be sought elsewhere, in rallies for example. In the 1980s Lancia was the expert in these road races, forever the orphans of the Targa Florio (no longer held since 1977); it won the 1983 championship with the Rally 037. The turn of the Delta came in 1987 and it went on to win six consecutive world manufacturer's titles and five driver's titles up until 1992. However, Lancia officially stopped racing at the end of 1991 due to high management costs and the concentration of economic efforts by the Fiat Group to re-launch the Ferrari in Formula One and to sustain Alfa Romeo, which stood out during touring car races, initially with the 155 and later with the 156. Another successful year for prototype racing followed in 1993, a former specialty of Alfa Romeo in the seventies. The Ferrari 333SP Barchetta, entrusted to a team of private individuals including Giampiero Moretti, thrashed the United States in the IMSA Championship and represented the Ferrari *stallion's* image proudly overseas.

264 and 265 The Lancia
Delta S4 was the queen of
rallies. Two hundred units were
produced in a road-legal version
in 1985 so it could be type-
approved in Group B. It
immediately won in England
and was triumphant until the
next year when Group B was
eliminated. The race version was
equipped with a rear, centrally
positioned Abarth engine with
400 hp, an intercooler and
permanent four-wheel drive,
and its body was made with
composite materials.

CHAPTER 7

A global challenge involving emissions, consumption and size

S afety and the environment are the subjects at the forefront of this century. Countries emerging in terms of motorization, such as China and India, are experiencing great expansion. The policy of alliances and agreements continued in 2000: Renault and Nissan merged, as did Daimler (that is Mercedes, Maybach and Smart) and Chrysler (although they separated in 2007). BMW re-launched Mini, Land Rover and Jaguar went to Tata (India) and Fiat went to GM for engines and chassis but also collaborated with Tata and with BMW through Alfa Romeo or through the acquisition of 35 percent of Chrysler, which opened the overseas market to the 500 and Alfa Romeo. The Indian company also obtained a piece of Italian automobile history by acquir-

ing Zagato. It is a terrible time for car designers considering that Bertone is in receivership and the Pininfarina family has left the helm of the historic company. Then the great economic crisis of 2008, sparked in the US by sub-prime mortgages combined with the extremely high price of crude oil, brought economies around the world to their knees, resulting in a recession with a particularly strong effect on the auto industry. The Big Three Ford, GM and Chrysler are in a deep crisis, and are clinging to aid from the government of newly elected president Barack Obama. In terms of product evolution, this is a period of great comebacks: Mini and Fiat 500 above all, followed by the new Volkswagen Beetle and retro models like Chrysler's PT Cruiser. Certain phenomena have been confirmed, such as sports utility vehicles and

crossovers and the off-road vehicle with coupe-like performance is outfitted like a large sedan, has the modularity and functionality of a minivan and the load capacity of a station wagon. But these are also times of anti-pollution legislation, years in which the sale of diesel vehicles exceeds gas vehicles, when LPG and methane-operated vehicles are distributed, the era of the first standard hybrids and continuous experimentation with electric and hydrogen vehicles. Huge steps are also being taken in terms of active and passive safety. Front, side, rear and knee-level airbags have become common in cars as have ABS, safety-belt pre-tensioners and pro-grammed-deformation bodies in the event of crashes to protect the driver and passenger compartments and their occupants. And then there is downsizing, both in terms of propulsion systems with low-powered, high-performing engines thanks to double boosting, and contained consumption and emissions. There have also been reductions in terms of size, with increasingly compact vehicles whose accessories, outfitting and five-star performance resolve the problem of mobility in increasingly crowded and polluted urban centers, while still providing maximum comfort for average-distance trips. The future will certainly be dictated by 'small is beautiful'; speed, low consumption, possibly a hybrid and in any event, with reduced emissions and all at an affordable price.

266-267 The 2002 Ferrari Enzo was produced in honor of the Drake and also to continue the series of vehicles (288 Gto, F40 and F50), which in Maranello represented the highest level of technology developed for racing. It was modified for a road-legal model that was also at home on the track. In truth, it was a single-seater masked as an automobile with sharp shapes, an abundance of high-tech materials (even part of the steering wheel was carbon), an F1 transmission and excellent mechanics, along with a V12 6.0L (5998 cc), 660 hp engine that could reach 217 mph (350 km/h). A total of 399 units were sold at a price of 660,000 Euros.

208 and 209. The new Fiat 500 made its debut on July 4, 2007, exactly 50 years after the original, adopting the stylistic elements of its ancestors to the modern world. Made in the Polish factory of Tychy, the new city car par excellence was equipped with the same chassis as the Nuova Panda and the Nuova Ford Ka. It is 12 feet (3.55 m) long (the first was 10

feet or 2.97 m long), very glamorous and intends to be a trend-setter, just like the Mini. An enviable series of accessories, in addition to a complete range of engines – including the more "muscular" Abarth 135 hp version (the previous version only had 27 hp, which was double that of the standard version) – allow it to be personalized in many ways.

"F" like Ferrari and Formula One

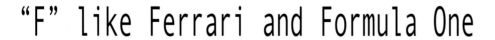

270 Michael Schumacher in a Ferrari attempting to qualify on the Interlogos Circuit for the Formula One Brazilian Grand Prix in 2006 (above) and during the race's second pit stop on the 47th lap

(below). The German driver finished fourth and drove the fastest lap. This driver also concluded his brilliant career in Brazil at the age of 37, having spent the previous 15 years winning Formula One races.

Excessive power in the rainbow-colored circus influenced mass production, which moved ahead at full speed. From up above, Ferrari could not have asked for more. Between 2000 and 2004, Formula One driver's and manufacturer's world titles enriched a showcase that had not been opened in 21 years. Schumacher was the hero of these successes, but Barrichello also contributed to the victories in the manufacturer's champi-

onships. Schumacher left the scene in 2006, but the red cars conquered the driver's world championship in 2007 through Raikkonen. After the findings by the Federation Internationale de l'Automobile about the spy story engineered by McLaren that was detrimental to the racing team in Maranello, it also went on to win the manufacturer's title in 2008. One link between the track and road was a model that made its debut in 2002,

called Enzo. The homage paid to the Drake was personified in a racing car equipped with the maximum technology gained in Formula One. Majestic and angular – like the nature of its founder – its profile was also inspired by the single-seaters and it was equipped with a V12, 6.0L (6000 cc), 660 hp engine. Even the essential, hi-tech driver and passenger compartment (with seats made of carbon) smelled of Formula One.

270-271 *Kaiser Schumy seen from above during the San Marino Grand Prix at Imola in 2006. He started the race in pole position and went on to win it in his Ferrari 248 F1 single-seater, the same vehicle used to end his unrepeatable Formula One career with seven titles, as demonstrated by the seven stars on his helmet.*

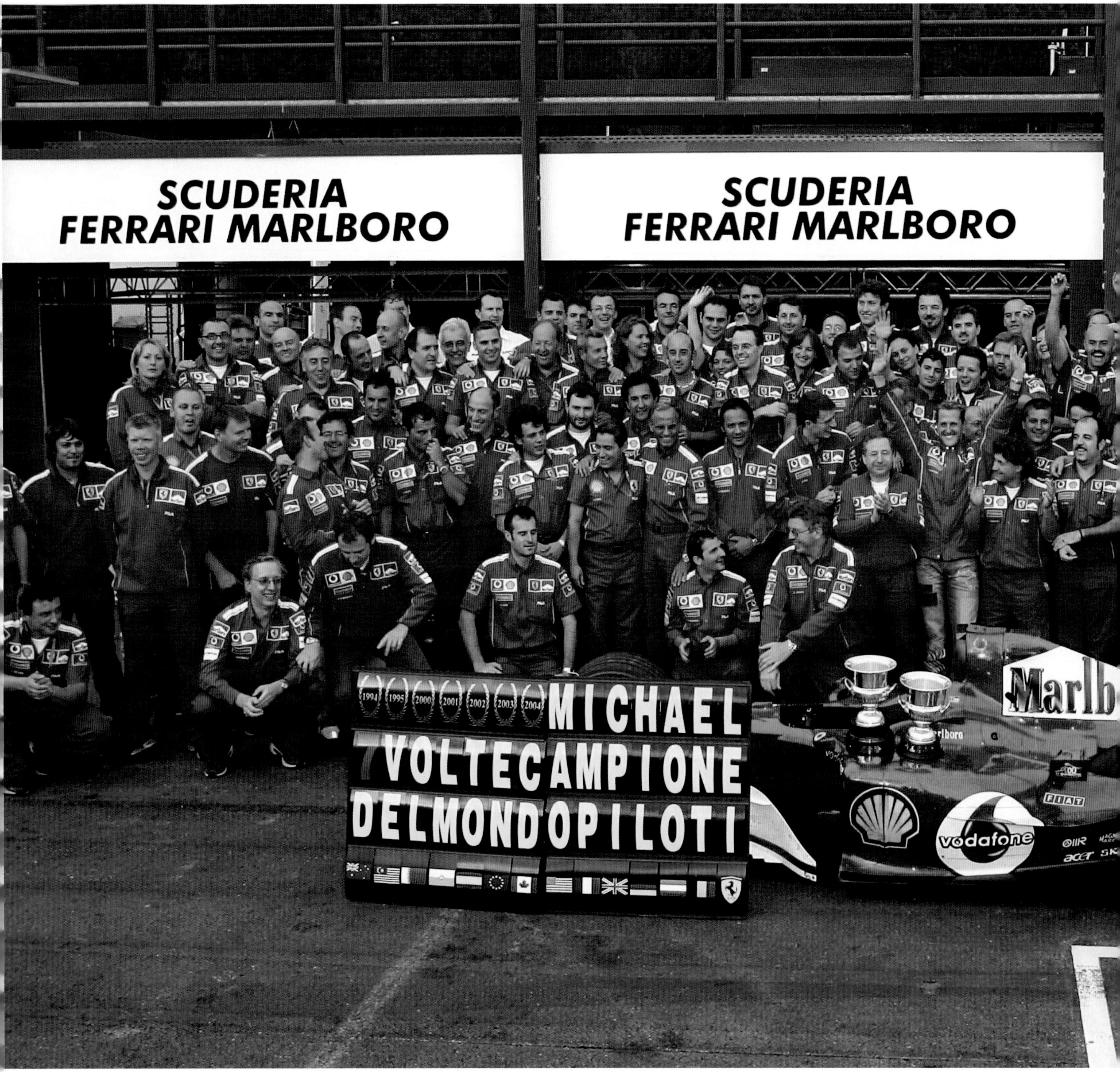

SCUDERIA
FERRARI MARLBORO
SCUDERIA
FERRARI MARLBORO
1994 1995 2000 2001 2002 2003 2004
MICHAEL
7 VOLTE CAMPIONE
DEL MONDO PILOTI
Marlb
vodafone
FIAT
acer

272-273 The complete Ferrari Team in front of the pits celebrates Michael Schumacher, who won his seventh Driver's World Championship at the Belgian Grand Prix in Spa-Francorchamps, before the season had even finished. His success was made possible by the team.

273 top Ferrari Chairman Luca Cordero di Montezemolo embraces race-car driver Michael Schumacher at the Italian Grand Prix in Monza in 2006. The driver announced he would retire from Formula One racing, but remain as a consultant.

273 bottom Ferrari driver Michael Schumacher celebrates a home victoryon the podium of the European Grand Prix at Germany's historic Nürburgring circuit.

As for road GTs, the 612 Scaglietti made its debut in 2004 to honor the great Modenese master and panel beater Sergio, who shaped some of the most beautiful Ferraris. The 612 is appropriate to Modenese car designer who died in 1975 and the results are an elegant, sophisticated, 100 percent aluminum grand touring car with a V12, 5.7L (5700 cc), 540 hp engine. This classy vehicle is extremely comfortable and easy to handle and was later also proposed in a version equipped with a paddle-shift system with steering-wheel controls like the ones used in Formula One. It was also presented in a special, limited edition on the occasion of the brand's 60th anniversary in 2007 (60 units were made). The 612 had great commercial success considering that its delivery time exceeded a year, and continued the wave of strongly requested spot-on models – even in rich new markets like the Far East. Among these

274-275 This Ferrari 612 Scaglietti is a marvelous example of style and technique. Sixty units of the special version shown here were produced to celebrate the brand's 60th anniversary. The vehicle made its debut in 2004 in honor of the car designer who designed some of the most beautiful cars at Maranello. An authentic grand touring 2+2 seater, this vehicle was produced in aluminum and was equipped with a V12 5.7L (5748 cc), 540 hp engine that could reach 196 mph (315 km/h).

276-277 The Scuderia was the racing and lightened (it weighed 220 lbs – 100 kg – less) version of the Ferrari F430 and made its debut in 2007, three years after the first version, which gave light to a new generation of Ferraris after the 360 Modena. The Scuderia stood out for its burnished rims, wonderful, visible, yellow Brembo brake calipers and 510 hp.

was the 360 Spider in 2000 and its 2004 replacement, the F430, including the Spider and Scuderia versions, which started a new generation of models with a V8 propulsion system. The 612 aside, the subject of 12 cylinders was encompassed by the 2005 575 Superamerica, which as the name indicates, was looking to conquer the market overseas. A carbon, hard-top system rotated to reveal the vehicle and to transform it into an open sports car. This was one of its main features, in addition to being the fastest convertible in the world (199 mph, 320 km/h). The FXX was released the same year as the 575. Thirty unapproved units were experimented with on the track and were destined to follow a program involving racing and test drivers with a supercar that combined the technology of the Enzo with the latest developments from Ferrari's research and development and its suppliers, such as Brembo.

Finally, 2008 was dedicated to the 599 GTB Fiorano, with a V12 engine taken from the Enzo and magnetorheologic suspension, which contained fluid in the shock absorbers able to instantly modify the vehicle's tilt. It was also reminiscent of and dedicated to the California, the unforgettable vehicle characterized as a coupe-convertible, produced between 1957-1963 and still the queen of sales today at auctions. Its rigid top disappears in 14 seconds with an automated mechanism and transforms the coupe into a convertible for four people. This Ferrari's performance is also excellent, resulting not just in "wind blowing in your hair" but more of a true whirlwind, considering its powerful V8 4.3L (4296 cc), 460 hp engine, which guarantees a maximum speed of 193 mph (310 km/h) and acceleration of 0 to 62 miles (0 to 100 km) in just four seconds.

278-279 The Ferrari California made its debut in 2008 and is reminiscent of the Maranello, one of the manufacturer's iconic models. The first convertible Ferrari with a metal top, making it either a coupe or convertible, was equipped with a V8 4.3L (4296 cc), 460 hp engine that could reach up to 193 mph (310 km/h) with the "wind blowing in your hair".

Alfa Romeo, centennial tests including the return
of the 8C and the creation of Brera and MiTo

The new century started under the sign of the Biscione. To commemorate its 100th anniversary, the Fiat Group wanted Alfa Romeo to consolidate its legacy, which included sportiness, determination, performance and Milanese essence. The anniversary will be celebrated in 2010 with the return of the automaker to Milan whose logo includes the city's symbol, a red cross, and the Visconti Biscione. A significant hand is provided by races, which continued in the wake of the 155. In 2000 and 2001, the 156 GTA won the Marche Championship and the European Touring Car Manufacturer's Championship. The 156 ST won the driver's title in 2003 with Gabriele Tarquini, while the team title went to the Autodelta race team, which withdrew in 2007 when Alfa Romeo officially left motor racing. Its slogan's sporty heart also beats strong in mass production. Making their debuts were the 147, to replace the 145 and 146, in 2000, the elegant GT coupe by Bertone in 2003, the Crosswagon Q4 in 2004 and the successful 159 in 2005 (and the Sportwagon the following year), which didn't at all mourn the 156. Instead it was able to assert itself in the crowded, tough segment of mid-size sedans and station wagons with its strong personality, thanks to a successful sporty profile, high-performing engines and sophisticated outfitting. In 2005 it was the turn of the Brera, designed by Giugiaro and manufactured by Pininfarina. This seductive coupe's strong shape and aggressive look pleased the public. Heir to the GTV, it conquered many lost Alfa enthusiasts, as did the 2007 Spider, which drew from the Brera's stylistic elements and was presented as a convertible with the classic textile top rather than the hard tops that were common at the time.

280 and 281 Alfa enthusiasts put on their best smiles when they saw the Brera at its debut in 2005. This sporty line was in keeping with the philosophy and unique values of an automobile manufacturer like Alfa Romeo, which waved the Italian flag in the world of international races before Ferrari and established itself in the market with its sporty DNA. This aggressive-looking yet elegant coupe replaced the Gtv. The engine measured up too, including a five-cylinder turbo diesel, 24-valve engine with 2.4L (2400 cc) Common Rail injection. The Brera also led to the 2007 Spider.

282 top *The Alfa Romeo MiTo (the name is a play on words related to the journey that united the Milanese – Mi – and the essence of the Biscione* trademark with the parent company Fiat in Turin or Torino – To) *is the first result of the renewed range inspired after the 8C in terms of style and sportiness and was, naturally, a very affordable model.*

282-283 *Alfa Romeo decided to create a muscle car similar to the 8C Competizione that measured up to the important name it was given. The 8C 2300 and 2900 were memorable in races while Juan Manuel Fangio's 6C Competizione won the 1950 Mille Miglia. The 8C made its debut in 2007 and only 500 units were produced. It was the ultimate expression of Alfa Romeo style and mechanics and became the benchmark for other models in the range. It was equipped with a 450-hp V8 4.7L (4691 cc) engine that allowed it to reach speeds in excess of 186 mph (300 km/h).*

But the essence of Alfa Romeo reached its climax with the 8C, which was mass-produced after the concept car was presented in 2003 at the Frankfurt Auto Show, where it was very successful. The name was cumbersome and it drew on an Alfa icon from the 1930s, but this new G1 knew how to best take from and reinterpret the noble history of this Milanese trademark. The front end was reminiscent of the unforgettable 33 road-legal version and it was equipped with a carbon body and a powerful V8, 4.7L (4700 cc), 450 hp engine taken from Maserati. The sound of the engine was music to the ears of fine automobile lovers and the vehicle's seductive, harmonious profile conquered all. The 8C was Alfa Romeo's new course and in 2008 generated the MiTo, a name that, in Italian, can also be read Milan-Turin. It was the new entry model in the Alfa Romeo range. Compact, with shapes inspired by the 8C, even this small Alfa abounded with personality and was an attempt to conquer those young motorists looking to German cars who knew very little of Alfa Romeo and its glorious history. The 149, replacing the 147, is also highly anticipated and will make its debut in 2009, as will the Giulia, which will replace the 159 and mark Alfa Romeo's return to the United States.

Lancia's 100 years and the return of the Delta

LANCIA

THESIS
THESIS *THESIS*
THESIS *THESIS*
THESIS *THESIS*
THESIS *THESIS*
THESIS *THESIS*

For Lancia, as with Alfa Romeo, the turn of the century has led to re-launching products with a series of models accompanying the Turinese automaker towards its 100th anniversary, which was celebrated in 2006. The goal was to put together a comprehensive, competitive range that can re-conquer those foreign markets where Lancia is practically non-existent. The Thesis made its debut in 2002, a high-tech flagship with sophisticated shapes and a tail end characterized by LED light units. The Phedra minivan, heir to the Z, also made its debut as a great traveler outfitted to match the level of the brand. The Ypsilon was created the following year in the wake of the successful Y. Its tail end is reminiscent of the Ardea and as always, the interior is very sophisticated and exclusive, resulting in a vehicle that is highly regarded, especially by young people and women. The year 2004 saw the turn of the compact minivan Musa, which was restyled in 2007 to meet market trends that sought compact, multifunctional vehicles. Unlike its cousin, the Idea, the Musa's advantages included exclusive interiors and accessories. Finally, 2008 was the year of the new Delta, a worthy expression of Lancia's new course after its 100th anniversary. Vincenzo Lancia would have liked this vehicle because it broke out of the classic mold and had cutting-edge shapes (a sporty sedan with the combined nature of both a small minivan and a small station wagon), but without ties to past models, and sophisticated and refined high-tech equipment and outfitting materials.

284 top The Thesis was a Lancia flagship and made its debut in 2002. Several of its stylistic elements, such as the front headlamps, were inspired by the Aurelia. It received its elegance from the Flaminia and its performance from the Fulvia.

284 bottom The nonconformist Lancia Delta had unique yet elegant shapes and proportions in accordance with those characteristics pursued by Vincenzo Lancia. It made its debut in 2008.

285 Always glamorous, the 2003 Lancia Ypsilon continued the honorable career of previous models as an exclusive, compact, attractive, accessorized, reliable and high-performing vehicle. It should almost belong to a higher category.

MOVIMENTO IMPRESSIONISTA.

The new Fiat 500 and the Campagnola

The new millennium did not begin in the best of ways for the Fiat Group, which found itself facing a new and serious crisis in 2002 (the worst in its history), the death of Gianni Agnelli the following year and a product range struggling with both old (French, German and Japanese) and new (Korean) competition. Corporate restructuring with Luca Cordero di Montezemolo as chairman, John Elkann as deputy chairman and Sergio Marchionne as president resulted in a re-launching of the Group's five brands and an advantageous agreement with GM. Each brand had its own, precise identity. Fiat specialized in versatile vehicles with enviable city-car know-how, Lancia's DNA was based on luxury and being on the cutting-edge, Alfa Romeo was synonymous with sportsmanship and performance, Fiat's commercial vehicles were always highly regarded, even abroad, and Abarth was re-launched through more "muscular" versions such as the Grande Punto and Nuova 500. Once again the automobile became the Group's core business and confirmed the arrival of investments, which resulted in new successful models in addition to paying greater attention to emerging markets in order to meet the very strong competition in Italy and Europe. This led to plants in Brazil and Argentina and the debut of a world car in the Palio. The new course of the models started with the Panda and continued with the Croma, the Grande Punto, the Sedici and the Bravo. These automobiles – including the multi-purpose Doblò and the compact minivan Idea – all took chunks of both the Italian and European markets. The presentation of the new 500 in 2007 was particularly strong and oc-

curred exactly 50 years after the debut of the first generation, which had given life to the *Made in Italy* city-car par excellence. An operation involving style drawn from the shapes of the original model moved the new 500 up a notch to become a trendy, cool vehicle that left its original austerity behind in favor of sophisticated outfitting and complete accessories. This made it an excellent alternative to the Mini because it cost less and, moreover, is an Italian brand, despite being manufactured in Poland. The 500's success reached beyond Italy's borders and more than 270,000 units had been sold within a year. Station wagon and convertible versions are expected to hit the streets in 2009. Well deserved success for this vehicle, along with the new 2003 Panda, highly regarded and reliable with its mini minivan shape, the 2005 Grande Punto and 2008 Bravo, which competed fearlessly against such heavyweights as the Volkswagen Golf, brought smiles back to the faces of Fiat's top management and profits to the Group's balance sheets. There was also the Croma, whose station wagon shape and minivan-like stature became highly regarded by fleets and even requested by English taxi companies. Even the short Ulysse minivan cut out its own niche equal to that of the compact SUV Sedici developed together with Suzuki. There was also room for a tough, pure off-road vehicle developed based on the Iveco Massif, which brought back a historic name dear to Fiat. The square, unstoppable Campagnola made its debut in 2008, including a stylistic evolution with corresponding technological updates with respect to the 1951 model (which was also later reassessed in 1974).

286 left It was time for a Fiat SUV and in 2006 it presented its Sedici, developed with Suzuki and produced by the Hungarian plant owned by the Japanese company.

286 right The Nuova Bravo made its debut in 2007 with a unique and captivating appearance. It also had a broad range of gas (with the unprecedented turbo T-Jet engines) and diesel engines.

286-287 The Nuova 500 was a functional car that captured the public (270,000 units were sold in the first year). It implemented the latest technology, which was applied to the mechanics and the comfort and safety features.

287 bottom left In 2005 the Grande Punto was a model with sophisticated and captivating shapes and a broad range of engines, including an Abarth version.

287 bottom right The Nuova Panda made its debut in 2003 and replaced the previous model, whose various generations had been present for some 23 years. It is manufactured in Poland as is the Nuova 500.

Maserati and Lamborghini, the other side of the Made in Italy dream cars

After it was sold to Ferrari, Maserati was reborn with a suitable product policy, considered necessary by chairman Luca Cordero di Montezemolo. This policy included Ferrari support in terms of the technology used on the Tridente's models. The results were a return by the Modenese automaker to its glorious past. After "laying its first stone" with the 3200 GT, the Spyder and Coupe debuted in 2001-2002 with a V8, 4.2L (4200 cc), 390 hp inlet engine and technical solutions like an intelligent suspension system that instantly adapts to the driving style, or the Cambiocorsa versions with Formula One-style transmission. The 3200 GT was produced until 2002 and was replaced in 2005 by the 8V GranSport, which also had a V8, 4.2L (4200 cc) inlet engine and a more traditional tail end with respect to the model it replaced. The MC12 was from the previous year and was created for GT races, but 50 road-legal units were also manufactured, and offered the best of Ferrari and Maserati in terms of technology. This 600,000 euro race car took to the road with a carbon and Nomex fiber chassis, and a V12, 5.6L (5600 cc), 660 hp engine that could reach 205 mph (330 km/h). But the two models that marked the turning point and brought back great success, not only in terms of sales but also a credit balance in 2007, were the Quattroporte and the GranTurismo. The first is a flagship with a seductive, sporty profile designed by Pininfarina (Andrea Pininfarina died in 2008 following a road accident), with excellent engineering and a sumptuous interior that could be further personalized. Equipped with a V8, 4.2L (4200 cc), 400 hp inlet engine, it was also available, as of 2007, in a DuoSelect version with a paddle-shift system used in Formula One, the Automatica version with a classic automatic transmission with a converter, and the

sporty GT. The 2007 GranTurismo (which also became an S as of 2008; an open sports car version is envisaged for 2010), is the Maserati par excellence. Thanks to Pininfarina, this car pays tribute to the brand's noble history, with references to the A6GCS coupe but especially with its both sporty and sensual appearance. It is harmonious yet determined and best

expresses the concept of grand touring. It is fast but comfortable and spacious enough for four people to be pampered by the on-board electronics and excellent leather and materials. The V8, 4.2L (4200 cc) and 405 hp inlet engine pushes hard: speeds of 177 mph (285 km/h) are easy to reach, thanks to its mechanical structure and division of weight, making it a pleasure

288-289 and 289 top Designed by Pininfarina and produced by Touring, the fifth series of the Quattroporte made its debut in 2003 with sporty, aggressive shapes. The driver and passenger compartment is very large and can be personalized. Elegant but also a performer, the Quattroporte comes equipped with a V8 4.2L (4244 cc), 400 hp engine capable of reaching 171 mph (275 km/h).

Lamborghini has also been re-launched, but this time thanks to Audi. The Volkswagen Group also has the Bugatti among its dream cars and has produced the Veyron 16.4 with a 16-cylinder, W, 8.0L (8000 cc), 1001 hp engine that can reach 253 mph (407 km/h) and costs 1.1 million euros (plus taxes), and the Murcielago – heir to the Diablo – which made its debut in 2001. It still bears the name of a bull, and in this case it is a bull spared by the bullfighter due to its strength. Designed by Bertone and developed by Audi designer Luc Donckerwolke, it was up to the mark's standard and had the design of a supercar, doors that opened upwards, four-wheel drive, and a rear, central 12-cylinder, 6.2L (6200 cc), 580 hp engine that reached a maximum speed of

203 mph (330 km/h). In 2006 it was the turn of the Roadster with a new 640 hp engine, followed by the LP640, with its propulsion system placed longitudinally in the back. In 2003 came the "small" Gallardo (the name was taken from a breeder of fighting bulls), designed by Giugiaro's Italdesign and produced by Donckerwolke. It was more compact than the Murcielago, was equipped with a V10, 5.0L (5000 cc), 530 hp engine and one was also issued to the Italian Police. The Spider made its debut in 2005, two years after the Superleggera (it weighed only 3130 lbs, 1420 kg) and the LP 560-4 Coupe and Spyder appeared in 2008. The success achieved by the brand of the bull was now international. Its leading market was the United States

and 30 percent of the overseas deliveries ended up in southern California. The wild car Reventón (the bull that killed bullfighter Felíx Guzmán in 1943) made its debut in 2007 in carbon fiber. Its shapes and outfitting, especially the driver's compartment, were clearly inspired by fighter planes. Only 20 units were produced, featuring carbon ceramic brakes and a 650 hp engine that reached 211 mph (340 km/h) and accelerated from 0-62 mph (0-100 km/h) in 3.4 seconds – all for the price of one million euros. Another Lambo, the Estoque, was presented in a concept version the following year at the Paris Auto Show. It was the precursor to a captivating, trendy four-door, four-seater sedan-coupe and the first vehicle of its kind in the brand's history.

Pagani also continued its adventure with high-performing super cars and in 2007 the Zonda S7.3 made its debut with a 12-cylinder Mercedes-Amg, 7.3L (7300 cc), 555 hp engine. Both coupe and roadster flaunted a carbon-fiber bodywork on a tubular molybdenum chrome steel chassis. There were also the 605 hp or 650 hp (Clubsport version) F coupes or roadsters, which were dedicated to Juan Manuel Fangio. Finally, the R was requested as a one-off special by an American client and later six other units were produced and personalized for as many owners. This road-legal racing car was equipped with Avional suspension, a gas tank used for jets and 720 hp that pushed it to 261 mph (420 km/h).

290-291 Charming, sporty, powerful: This Lamborghini Murcielago, named after a bull in keeping with the brand's tradition, made its debut in 2001 and was the first model produced under Audi management. The vehicle is the best of German technology combined with high-tech materials, mobile body elements, four wheel drive and a V12 6.2L (6192 cc), 580 hp engine that has a maximum speed of 205 mph (330 km/h). Two thousand and six was the turn of the Roadster and the Lp640, which stands for longitudinale posteriore or rear longitudinal (in reference to the engine) and horsepower.

291 top The year 2003 saw the turn of the Lamborghini Gallardo, designed by Giugiaro's Italdesign. It was a more compact model than the Murcielago and its doors did not open upwards as they did on other models. Its engine was also reduced and only had 10 cylinders (5.0L or 4961 cc) and 530 hp, which rest firmly on the ground thanks to four-wheel drive and a top speed of 196 mph (315 km/h). The Spider made its debut in 2005, two years after the Superleggera, while the LP 560-4 Coupe and Spider made theirs in 2008.

292-293 This is the best expression of grand touring in the new millennium. This Maserati was presented in 2007 and just had to be called Gran Turismo. It is a super fast and comfortable vehicle for four with 405 hp, which can reach high speeds but is also at ease at touring speeds. It is the ultimate in terms of luxury and exclusiveness, and the essence of what a grand touring vehicle should be. Like the Quattroporte, this marvelous vehicle brought Maserati back to its former, well-deserved splendor.

294-295 This vehicle was one of the main attractions at the 2008 Villa d'Este Concours d'Elégance. It is a Touring Superleggera Maserati A8GCS with the stylistic elements of the famous 1950s A6GCS, remodelled in a coupe based on the GranTurismo.

AUTHORS

Giorgetto Giugiaro, one of the most famous Italian designers, works in many fields, but became internationally renowned largely as a result of his work in the automobile field. He has designed exclusive sports cars and popular road models such as the Alfetta GT/GTV, the Ferrari 250 GT Bertone, the Fiat Panda and the Fiat Punto. In 1999 Giorgetto Giugiaro was honored with the title "Car Designer of the Century" and in 2002 he was admitted into the Automotive Hall of Fame.

Enzo Rizzo is a professional journalist. He is the sub-editor of two magazines, *Monsieur* and *Spirito diVino,* and he also works for *Il Giornale* and *Flotte&Finanza.* Together with his colleague, Giuseppe Guzzardi, he has compiled the multimedia production, *Alfa Romeo: a Century of Racing* and he has written *Convertibles. History and Evolution of Dream Cars* and *Motor Racing. The Drivers and Their Machines* for Edizioni White Star.

BIBLIOGRAPHY

Valerio Castronovo, *Agnelli,* Ed. Utet

Griffith Borgeson, *Alfa Romeo, i creatori della leggenda,* Giorgio Nada Editore

Larry Edsal, *Auto e design, i maestri dello stile,* Edizioni White Star

Giuseppe Guzzardi, Enzo Rizzo, *Cabriolet,* Edizioni White Star

Giuseppe Guzzardi, Enzo Rizzo, *Cento anni di automobilismo sportivo,* Edizioni White Star

Giorgio Mori, *Il capitalismo industriale in Italia,* Ed. Editori Riuniti

L'auto 2007, sintesi statistica anni 1998-2007, UNRAE (Italian National Union of Foreign Car Representatives)

Alberto Bellucci, *L'automobile italiana dal 1918 al 1943,* Ed. Laterza

O. Sessa, A. Bruni, M. Clarke, F. Paolini, F. Manzoni *L'automobile italiana, tutti i modelli dalle origini a oggi* Giunti Editore

Valerio Castronovo, *L'industria italiana dall'800 a oggi,* Ed. Mondatori

AA.VV., *L'industria italiana nel mercato mondiale dalla fine dell'800 alla metà del 900,* Fiat historic archives

Museum of Modern and Contemporary Art of Trento and Rovereto, *Mitomacchina, il design dell'automobile: storia, tecnologia, futuro,* Skira Editore

Quattroruote, various issues, Ed. Domus

Tutte le Alfa Romeo, 1910-2000, Editoriale Domus

Tutte le Fiat, 1899-2000, Editoriale Domus

Tutte le Lancia, 1907-2002, Editoriale Domus

Tutto Ferrari, la prima raccolta di tutti i modelli Ferrari, Mondadori

ACKNOWLEDGMENTS

The publishing house would like to thank: Lorenza Cappello and Umberto Gorio - Italdesign - Giugiaro Spa; Paolo in Taranto - Zagato; Gianni Cattaneo - Automobile Club Archives of Milan - Monza National Speedway; Matthias Enzinger - Audi AG - Audi Media Services; Alessandro Brioschi - Iso Millennium committee - Bresso; Uberto Pietra - Carrozzeria Touring Superleggera srl; Fiat AutoPress; Automobile Club Turin

INDEX

PHOTO CREDITS

Pages 1, 2-3 Ron Kimball/www.kimballstock.com
Pages 4-5, 6-7, 8-9, 10-11 Fotostudio Zumbrunn
Page 13 courtesy of the Italdesign Giugiaro S.p.a
Pages 14-15 Ron Kimball/www.kimballstock.com
Pages 16-17, 18-19 Fotostudio Zumbrunn
Pages 20-21, 22-23 Ron Kimball/ www.kimballstock.com
Pages 24-25 Rue des Archives
Pages 26-27 Archivio pgmedia.it
Page 27 David Lees/Corbis
Page 28 courtesy of the Audi AG/Audi Media Services
Pages 28-29 Bettmann/Corbis
Pages 30-31 Mary Evans Picture Library
Page 31 Rue des Archives
Pages 32-33 courtesy of the Fiat AutoPress
Page 33 left, 33 right Rue des Archives
Page 34, 34-35 Archivio Storico Fiat
Pages 36-37 Rue des Archives
Page 37 top, 37 bottom Negri, Brescia/Corbis
Pages 38-39 Fotostudio Zumbrunn
Page 39 courtesy of the Fiat AutoPress
Pages 40-41 Mary Evans Picture Library
Pages 42-43 Ron Kimball/www.kimballstock.com
Page 43 Hulton-Deutsch Collection/Corbis
Pages 44-45 Photoservice Electa/Akg Images
Page 45 Mary Evans Picture Library
Pages 46-47, 47 Negri, Brescia/Corbis
Pages 48-49 Roger Viollet/Archivi Alinari, Firenze
Page 49 top Mary Evans Picture Library
Page 49 bottom Museo Nicolis
Page 50 top Archivio Negri, Brescia
Page 50 bottom Museo Nicolis
Pages 50-51 Archivio Negri, Brescia
Pages 52-53 Corbis
Page 53 Museo Nicolis
Page 54 top left, 54 top right Archivio Storico Alfa Romeo
Page 54-55 John Lamm/Transtock/Corbis
Pages 56 top, 56 bottom courtesy of the Automobile Club Torino
Pages 56-57 Hulton Archive/Getty Images
Page 58 National Motor Museum
Pages 58-59 Corbis
Page 60 Roger Viollet/Archivi Alinari, Firenze
Pages 61, 62-63 Hulton-Deutsch Collection/ Corbis
Pages 63 top, 63 bottom Rue des Archives
Page 65 Archivio Storico Fiat
Pages 66-67 Bettmann/Corbis
Pages 67 top, 67 center, 67 bottom Museo Nicolis
Pages 68, 68-69 Andrea Jemolo/Corbis
Pages 70-71, 71 top, 71 bottom Archivi Alinari, Firenze
Page 72 Rue des Archives
Page 73 top Archivio Negri, Brescia
Page 73 bottom Museo Nicolis
Pages 74, 74-75 Fotostudio Zumbrunn
Page 76 top Ricordi & C. Spa
Page 76 bottom Foto Archivio Cassetta
Page 77 top Ricordi & C. Spa
Page 77 bottom Foto Archivio Cassetta
Pages 78-79 Fotostudio Zumbrunn
Page 80 Fox Photos/Getty Images
Pages 80-81, 81 left, 81 right Rue des Archives
Page 82 Archivio Storico Fiat
Pages 82-83 Museo Nicolis
Pages 84 top, 84 center, 84 bottom, 84-85 Fotostudio Zumbrunn
Page 86 courtesy of the Fiat AutoPress
Page 87 DeA Picture Library, under licence to Alinari

Pages 88-89 Fotostudio Zumbrunn
Page 90 top Ist. Luce/Gestione Archivi Alinari, Firenze
Page 90 bottom National Motor Museum
Pages 90-91 FarabolaFoto
Page 91 Photoshot
Page 92 Rue des Archives
Pages 93, 94-95, 96 Fotostudio Zumbrunn
Pages 96-97 Klemantaski Collecion/Getty Images
Page 96 Photoservice Electa/Akg Images
Pages 98-99 Ron Kimball/www.kimballstock.com
Page 99 Publifoto/LaPresse
Page 100 National Motor Museum
Pages 101, 102 courtesy of the Fiat AutoPress
Page 103 Mary Evans Picture Library
Page 104 Archivio Storico Fiat
Page 105 Alferd Eisenstaedt/Time & Life Pictures/Getty Images
Pages 106, 106-107, 108-109, 110-111, 112-113, 113, 114-115, 115 left, 115 right Fotostudio Zumbrunn
Page 116 DeA Picture Library, under licence to Alinari
Pages 116-117 Fotostudio Zumbrunn
Pages 118-119 Ron Kimball/www.kimballstock.com
Pages 120-121 Bettmann/Corbis
Page 121 Sante Lusuardi/Ferrari SpA
Pages 122-123, 124-125, 125, 126-127 Fotostudio Zumbrunn
Page 128 Farabolafoto
Page 129 courtesy of the Zagato
Page 130 Farabolafoto
Page 131 Roger Viollet/Archivi Alinari, Firenze
Pages 132 top, 132 bottom, 133 Farabolafoto
Pages 134-135 Fotostudio Zumbrunn
Page 136 Farabolafoto
Pages 136-137 Bettmann/Corbis
Page 138 Fotostudio Zumbrunn
Pages 138-139 ANSA/Corbis
Pages 140-141, 141 Fotostudio Zumbrunn
Pages 142, 142-143 Ferrari SpA
Page 143 Zincografia Modenese/Ferrari SpA
Page 144 Fotostudio Zumbrunn
Page 145 top Hulton Archive/Getty Images
Pages 145 bottom, 146-147, 148-149, 150-151, 152-153 Fotostudio Zumbrunn
Page 154 top Archivio Storico Fiat
Page 154 bottom LaPresse
Page 155 Farabolafoto
Page 156 courtesy of the Fiat AutoPress
Pages 156-157 Fotostudio Zumbrunn
Pages 157, 158-159, 160 top courtesy of the Fiat AutoPress
Page 160 bottom National Motor Museum
Pages 161, 162 top, 162 bottom courtesy of the Fiat AutoPress
Page 163 Photoservice Electa/Akg Images
Page 164 Farabolafoto
Pages 164-165, 166-167 Fotostudio Zumbrunn
Page 167 courtesy of the Fiat AutoPress
Pages 168-169, 169 Foto Archivio Cassetta
Page 170 DeA Picture Library, under licence to Alinari
Pages 170-171 Fotostudio Zumbrunn
Page 172 top courtesy of the Fiat AutoPress
Page 172 bottom Fotostudio Zumbrunn
Page 173 courtesy of the Fiat AutoPress
Page 174 top Silvio Durante/LaPresse
Page 174 bottom Foto Archivio Cassetta
Page 175 top Silvio Durante/LaPresse
Page 175 bottom Car Culture/Getty Images
Page 176 Farabolafoto

Pages 176-177 courtesy of the Fiat AutoPress
Page 177 Bettmann/Corbis
Pages 178, 178-179, 179 Farabolafoto
Pages 180 left, 180 right, 180-181 Fotostudio Zumbrunn
Page 181 Farabolafoto
Page 182 top LaPresse
Page 182 bottom Bettmann/Corbis
Pages 182-183 Farabolafoto
Page 184 courtesy of the Fiat AutoPress
Pages 184-185 Fotostudio Zumbrunn
Pages 186-187 Fotostudio Zumbrunn
Pages 188, 189 Farabolafoto
Pages 190, 190-191 courtesy of the Fiat AutoPress
Pages 192 top, 192 bottom, 192-193, 193 bottom courtesy of the Italdesign Giugiaro S.p.a
Pages 194-195 Ron Kimball/www.kimballstock.com
Pages 196 top, 196 bottom Farabolafoto
Pages 196-197 Ron Kimball/www.kimballstock.com
Pages 198-199 Fotostudio Zumbrunn
Pages 200 top, 200 center Ferrari SpA
Pages 200-201, 202, 202-203 Fotostudio Zumbrunn
Page 203 Klemantaski Collecion/Getty Images
Pages 204-205 Ron Kimball/www.kimballstock.com
Page 206 Mike McLaren/Central Press/Hulton Archive/Getty Images
Pages 206-207 Oleksiy Maksymenko/ Photolibrary Group
Page 207 Hulton Archive/Getty Images
Page 208 Ron Kimball/www.kimballstock.com
Pages 208-209, 210-211, 211 Fotostudio Zumbrunn
Page 212-213 top courtesy of the Comitato ISO Rivolta Millenium, Bresso
Pages 212-213 Ron Kimball/www.kimballstock.com
Page 214 courtesy of the Fiat AutoPress
Pages 214-215, 215, 216-217 Fotostudio Zumbrunn
Pages 218-219 Ron Kimball/www.kimballstock.com
Page 219 Everett Collection/Contrasto
Pages 220 top, 220 bottom, 220-221 David Lees/Time & Life Pictures/Getty Images
Pages 222-223, 223 courtesy of the Fiat AutoPress
Page 224 LaPresse
Pages 224-225 Foto Archivio Cassetta
Page 225 LaPresse
Page 226 Bettmann/Corbis
Pages 226-227 Allsport UK/Allsport/Getty Images
Page 227 Schlegelmilch/Corbis
Pages 228, 229 courtesy of the Fiat AutoPress
Pages 228-229 Michael Steele/Getty Images
Pages 230-231 Ron Kimball/www.kimballstock.com
Pages 232 left, 232 right, 233 left, 233 right courtesy of the Fiat AutoPress
Pages 234-235, 236-237, 238-239 Ron Kimball/ www.kimballstock.com
Pages 240, 241 top, 241 bottom courtesy of the Italdesign Giugiaro S.p.a
Pages 242 top, 242 bottom, 242-243, 244-245, 245 top, 245 center, 245 bottom, 246 top, 246-247, 247 courtesy of the Fiat AutoPress
Pages 248-249, 249 Maserati SpA
Pages 250, 250-251, 251 courtesy of the Italdesign Giugiaro S.p.a
Pages 252, 252-253 Ron Kimball/ www.kimballstock.com
Pages 254-255, 256-257 Fotostudio Zumbrunn

Pages 258-259, 260-261 Ron Kimball/ www.kimballstock.com
Page 262 top Farabolafoto
Page 262 bottom Mark Thompson/ Allsport/Getty Images
Pages 262-263 Schlegelmilch/Corbis
Pages 264, 264-265, 265 courtesy of the Fiat AutoPress
Pages 266-267 Ron Kimball/www.kimballstock.com
Pages 268, 269 courtesy of the Fiat AutoPress
Page 270 top Mark Thompson/Getty Images
Pages 270 bottom, 270-271 Schlegelmilch/Corbis
Pages 272-273 Clive Rose/Getty Images
Page 273 top STR/epa/Corbis
Page 273 bottom Schlegelmilch/Corbis
Pages 274-275, 276-277, 278-279 Ron Kimball/ www.kimballstock.com
Page 280 courtesy of the Italdesign Giugiaro S.p.a
Pages 280-281 courtesy of the Fiat AutoPress
Page 281 courtesy of the Italdesign Giugiaro S.p.a
Pages 282, 282-283, 284 top, 284 bottom, 285, 286-287 courtesy of the Fiat AutoPress
Pages 288-289, 289 Maserati SpA
Pages 290-291, 291 Ron Kimball/ www.kimballstock.com
Pages 292-293 Maserati SpA
Pages 294-295 courtesy of the Carrozzeria Touring Superleggera srl
Page 300 National Motor Museum

Cover
1939 Maserati A6 GCS.
© Fotostudio Zumbrunn

Back Cover
Ferrari P4/5.
© Ron Kimball / www.kimballstock.com

vmb PUBLISHERS

VMB Publishers® is a registered trademark property of Edizioni White Star s.r.l.

© 2009, 2011 Edizioni White Star s.r.l.
Via Candido Sassone, 24
13100 Vercelli, Italy
www.whitestar.it

Translation: Donna St. John
Editing: James Morrison

ISBN: 978-88-540-1645-3
1 2 3 4 5 6   15 14 13 12 11

Printed in China

*300 The Fiat 500 was an
icon and a pioneer of the
modern city car. Likeable,
revolutionary and original, it
made its debut in 1957,
remained in production until
1975 and made a comeback
in 2007 in an entirely new
version inspired by the shapes
of the original model.*